THE ETHNOGRAPHY OF A SOCIAL WORK INTERN

Pollie Bith-Melander, PhD, MSW, ACSW, PPSC

Author's Tranquility Press
Marietta, Georgia

Copyright © 2022 by Pollie Bith-Melander.

All rights reserved. No part of this publication may be reproduced, distributed or transmitted in any form or by any means, including photocopying, recording, or other electronic or mechanical methods, without the prior written permission of the publisher, except in the case of brief quotations embodied in critical reviews and certain other noncommercial uses permitted by copyright law. For permission requests, write to the publisher, addressed "Attention: Permissions Coordinator," at the address below.

Pollie Bith-Melander/Author's Tranquility Press
2706 Station Club Drive SW
Marietta, GA 30060
www.authorstranquilitypress.com

Publisher's Note: This is a work of non-fiction.

Ordering Information:
Quantity sales. Special discounts are available on quantity purchases by corporations, associations, and others. For details, contact the "Special Sales Department" at the address above.

The Ethnography of a Social Work Intern/Pollie Bith-Melander
Paperback: 978-1-957546-01-8
eBook: 978-1-957546-02-5

Table of Contents

CHAPTER 1: Ready, Set, Go 5

CHAPTER 2: Ethnographic Fieldwork 34

CHAPTER 3: Case Presentations, Vicarious trauma, and Things That Trigger 43

CHAPTER 4: Minor Technicalities 61

CHAPTER 5: Career Change, Nonprofit Experiences, and Other Important Issues about Training 80

CHAPTER 6: MSW Program 100

CHAPTER 7: Clinical Supervisors 114

CHAPTER 8: The Post MSW Degree Experiences 132

CHAPTER 9: Subfields in Social Work 141

CHAPTER 10: Big Systems 153

Dedication

*For Sebastian, my son, who inspires me daily to
live life to the fullest.*

CHAPTER 1

Ready, Set, Go

It has been a long journey to become what I am today, and today I am most comfortable with myself because of the past experiences that I had the privilege of having. My journey started way before I was born. I could not say that I was destined to be in a foreign land, but it seems that way in hindsight. I came to the United States at a very young age without being literate in my native language or in English. So, knowing what I wanted to do in life was tricky. I did not have a role model nor did I grow up with a parent who had a traditional career, such as a medical doctor, teacher, or social worker. I had mentors later on in life, only after I was about to finish my bachelor degree at the University of California at Berkeley. However, growing up in a poor, urban community was almost a good thing for me in terms of learning the advantage of scarce resources. For example, it allowed me to participate in programs that existed mostly in poor communities, which helped inner-city kids like me thrive. I had such an opportunity when I attended high school. It was called Upward Bound then, but they call it something else now. So, my career path amounted to people's stories of people having successful careers of others in the field, but it was never directly with people that I knew. It was only meaningful to me later on in life when I began to explore some of the professional experiences myself in order to gain a more practical and deeper understanding of what to expect, especially those career choices that required intensive academic training. By the time I started my MSW training, I had enough experience to know what I needed to succeed, but mostly I was being skeptical, and at times cynical, about my surroundings. This began with being an intern as an undergraduate student.

Past Internship Experiences

My past experience in interning was limited to sporadic and self-imposed feel-good types of commitment with a focus on career explorations. I wanted to learn something about the different disciplines and fields in the social sciences prior to applying for post-baccalaureate programs, so I made calls to a few places to volunteer, to learn the ropes, so that I might achieve some of my career aspirations. This period predated googling and emailing. A phone book was our Google search machine then. I had some successes at getting placements but failed at others since I had no specific objectives or goals. I didn't know if I wanted to go to a medical or law school, or apply to a Professional Master's Program such as an MBA or MSW. My post internships before attending graduate schools were interesting to say the least. For example, I spent one month in a law office that provided immigration services and filed suits against various entities over personal injuries. The first two weeks of my time were filled with inspirations about being an attorney. It soured quickly since my volunteer job was filing and making phone calls to solicit if someone in the family had a car accident. I stayed on until the end of the internship. I did learn one thing that was informative, though. There were too many lawyers, and not all made it as attorneys practicing law the way they desired. But this dream stayed on through my undergraduate years of watching Ally McBeal, a TV show that glamorized attorneys, especially litigators. I was trapped again in my own whirlwind of career choices. Like any twenty something, I too was still lost. I learned more from the paralegal than the attorney who owned the firm. I first met him during the initial contact, so I'd know the location of his firm. Then, I saw him one more time, the last day of the internship. The knowledge of law and being an attorney came from my daily interactions with the paralegal and occasional law students who came to drop off depositions or other legal documents. This paralegal said that law and being an attorney involved reading and writing. I ran fast after hearing this from the woman. She resigned on the last day of my internship at the law firm. She was about to start her MBA program that fall.

The second internship, once again self-imposed, was at a county emergency room. The first night was slow. But the staff who worked at the emergency room warned me that things could change quickly. They told me to wait for a few days, like until mid-month or the end of the month. Three days into the internship, I was in over my head. Two men with gunshot wounds were delivered to the emergency room. More people with gunshot wounds showed up the following night. By the end of the week, I felt like I did not have anything left in my body to hold me upright. The sight of blood threw me off completely. I hyperventilated and was frightened by the scenes and wounds being so open and raw. Seeing blood and wounds caused me to empty everything out of my belly. I lasted one week. I vomited so much that I was triggered every time I saw that county hospital. I concluded that blood and I were fierce enemies.

My third internship took place over one Christmas holiday. I volunteered at a shelter, and my job was to find leftovers from food places and deliver them to the People's Park and similar places to give to homeless people. These were the best two weeks of any internship experience. It was in part due to an excellent mentor/field social worker whom I worked with for those two weeks. One of us would pick up food from a restaurant, social event, or other source, and we would track down homeless individuals at public places. My favorite spot was the People's Park near the UC Berkeley campus because it was a lively spot. It was not just homeless individuals who hung out at the park but all types of individuals. It was late during the afternoon when I made one of my rounds to the People's Park. I was still a student, completing my third year as an undergraduate, and I drove an old, generally unreliable, Jeep Cherokee. So, my unreliable car died on me during one of my rounds. The car came to a complete stop, and the police helped me by pushing the car to the side of the road, so that I would not cause traffic jam. While waiting for AAA, I tried the ignition and the car worked again. This car stall delayed my pickup and I ended up getting vegetarian leftovers instead of mixed dishes with meat and vegetables.

Since it was still dinnertime, I had my portions divided into individualized boxes, and those boxes were ready to be distributed to individuals at the park. I had twenty boxes, and they were good for twenty people. This was in the early 1990s and all these values on slow food movements were nowhere in sight yet. I gave to the first guy that I saw and he took it. He opened and threw the box in the trash. The next guy did the same thing. He threw the box in the trash. By the time I got to the third person, a woman in her 50s looked up at me and then stared at the box I was holding. She asked, "Is this vegetarian?" I smiled and politely answered, "Yes, how do you know?" She smiled back and said, "They threw the boxes away. They like meat. They only eat meat." So, I said to her, "This food is good for you. It is healthy." Her response made an impression on me even years later. She said, "Just because we are homeless, it does not mean that we are not picky when it comes to food." I ate a box and threw the rest away that day. One takeaway then was dignity. I didn't look back on these experiences when I plunged forward with graduate schools and research studies. My journey was in academia. I was traveling, teaching, and living until I went to work for the military. Then, things changed for me. Seeing veterans and soldiers struggle to deal with post-combat experiences was enough to shift my career trajectory. Somehow, I did not feel like I had a meaningful career as an academic after I spent some years seeing how they worked and struggled with post-military experiences. My contribution to society seemed meaningless and miniscule. Other personal changes in life led me to pursue a second master's degree. This time, I was determined to choose a career that offered me more satisfaction as a human being and a scholar.

The road that ultimately led me to a new career was quite challenging. I was already an established scholar and researcher in a different field. I knew it would be tough, but it was tougher than I anticipated. For one thing, no one seemed to appreciate my expertise in another field, and no one cared about it. For another, it seemed to work counter to my intentions when I tried to be helpful by offering my expertise. However, I still would not change any aspect of these experiences despite some of them being extremely challenging. I did march on like a good soldier by embracing the good things and remembering the bad things as lessons to be learned. This is what made my first experience as a social work intern rewarding and terrifying at the same time.

Choppy Starting Points

My first year of the MSW program got off to a rocky start, and it did not go as planned as far as field experience was concerned. I chose a school-based placement at a nonprofit agency that focused on independent living for people living with disabilities. It took me a while to secure an internship since I started the application process late and did not get to attend the internship fair at that time. I was given a list of agencies and told to call them to see who would still need an intern. I did so;

however, only a few of the agencies caught my attention. I needed a quick decision, so local government agencies would be out of the question unless I was an insider where people knew me personally. This meant working in an agency and knowing people with power to accommodate an intern. I called these places as a stranger without any affiliation. My chances and prospects of finding someone who was willing to do me a favor were slim to none. So, that only left me with any nonprofit agency that still needed interns.

Social work is not for everyone and knowing the agency is half of the battle. I am referring to placement experience or the unknown of the experience. Nonprofit agencies are interesting and seem to act similar to local government agencies but without the constraints of government's rules and regulations or bureaucracies. However, they have this "cowboy" approach to operations, depending on the size, scope, and duration of existence. I had enough experience from working in nonprofit agencies through the years as an undergraduate student and later as a graduate student to know when it was time to go and when it was time to say something to someone. But in the end, I came to the same conclusion. And that was to quickly run away from them before I went insane. Plus, I did not want to grow bitter about having a career. Running away seemed most logical until now, which I feel is imperative to share such experiences with those who are interested in going back to school or in having a second career. I endured for a few years in various nonprofit agencies post-MSW degree in order to confirm or disprove my own bias of working for a nonprofit agency.

Real Internships

Admit it! Being an intern sucks. Once you admit that you have a problem, the world seems brighter, as the cliché goes. Admitting you have a problem is the first step in recovery, which removes the elephant in the room. Some people may disagree with this belief, but the world does seem brighter for the people who admit that they have problems. I have always been conscious about being an intern. I am conscious because I believe that as an intern, we are most vulnerable in a work setting. We cannot be counted on as staff. We cannot be taken seriously because we are not being paid for the work. We cannot be expected to work long hours or be reliable because we have other obligations like taking on part-time jobs to pay bills or having to go home and take care of our own families. Being an intern seems more like being held in suspense for a job or a career. It is a suspension of motion, caught in between building skills and eventually having that ideal career and being recognized as a professional. Depending on one's view of this precarious position, however, I did not feel very useful as an intern. However, I tried to do my best to do these internship jobs as if I was getting paid.

I had four internships in total over the course of three years as a social work graduate student. The first one was when I enrolled as a full-time student in the full-time program in the California State University system. I was in the full-time program for a quarter. That internship also left me with an impression of good work. However, the field instructor was also an executive director of the agency. Her time was constrained in terms of guidance and teaching me (or us, since there were two of us then). I was pretty much left alone to help clients. The other one, in which I lasted for about two weeks, was also at a nonprofit agency. I was doing data entry as a social work intern. I do not have much to say about this particular internship except that it seemed I was only used for free labor. That left me with two major internships, and both made a lasting impression on my second career, as a social worker.

Year 1 Part-time Program Internship

My first real internship was at a Veterans Affairs medical facility. It was a good experience overall. Like any big system, though, it came with a certain reputation. I was told it provided good training opportunities for individuals who wanted to learn how to survive and learn the necessary skills to navigate a large system. It also came with a reputation of having larger-than-life staff and professionals and attracted certain types of personalities. So, it went with the treatment for poor interns.

Some of these professionals believed that they were larger than life and very important; therefore, interns deserved to be mistreated and preached to or continuously made to feel small. I felt this way during my entire time working as an intern, which for the entire year was three days a week of pain plus three hours of commute time. That was my experience at that facility.

While this was my first real internship, I had the privilege of meeting another intern who was also in the process of changing her career. She was a practicing attorney at the time before embarking on her MSW program and was about to start her internship at the VA just like me. We also received a small monthly stipend for the internship, but the VA demanded three days per week instead of the traditional first year requirement from a university's social work program of two days per week or sixteen hours per week. Typically, the VA only recruits final year students instead of newly inexperienced or first year students. It made sense as far as training and guidance is concerned. An agency gets more out of an advanced student for their money and time. I did not read about the VA's requirements when I contacted the coordinator and asked if it was too late for me to submit necessary documents and perhaps obtain an interview. In the email, I also introduced myself as a professional who was established in her own original field. I chose to change a career for two specific reasons: 1) Being in theater (war zone) with the military changed my perspective on how I wanted to live my life; and 2) I am looking to return to work with the military. I spent a few years conducting research studies for the military. It was important that I contribute to a big institution that I truly believed in. Our men and women in uniform deserve people committed to guiding them once they are out of the military and must participate in the civilian world.

My only plan was to explore all possibilities in both big and small institutions. I did not want to do an internship at the VA at the time because it was my first years in the MSW program, but I sent out an email anyway. I also had several other internship options, and the offers came through at that time. It was too late in the quarter. It had already started, and every student was supposed to have an internship locked in when I approached the VA social work coordinator. I initially hesitated to look into the VA for a simple reason. I did not want to commute two or more hours per day three days a week for the entire year. The VA's process of recruitment was slow. I knew that I had to start an internship immediately if I hoped to finish up to 480 hours for the academic year since the quarter had already started. So, I kept in contact with the VA coordinator, knowing that it was better to have options than to have to look for something else later on if things did not work out.

Providing myself options has always been my mantra in life as a career student. By this time, I had considered myself a career student since I had been in school for as long as I had been working, which meant I worked and went to school all of my adult life. I often did both and did them full-time for many years. So, I was used to developing exit strategies by this time in my life. I was never out of a job and never ran out of options because I engaged myself early in developing exit strategies. Testing the waters, figuratively speaking, came easy after a while. I usually knew if things would work out or not by the end of six weeks of being in a new job or whether I would stay for a while or leave immediately.

I started my first internship in the part-time program of a nonprofit agency near where I lived. It seemed to have everything that was important to me at the time. It was in a perfect location, nice and quiet. It was close to all of my favorite eateries. It was also close to all of my favorite shops. Since I enjoyed window shopping and have always viewed it as a part of my self-care, there was nothing anyone could say that would convince me this was less than ideal.

It took me less than five minutes to drive to the agency. I knew that it was easy for me to get dropped off since parking was horrendously expensive. I started my first day and was expected to meet the person who provided the training, and I assumed it was the same person who was going to supervise me. I was asked to wait at the entrance and did so for about thirty minutes before anyone came to greet me. The receptionist was nice and looked perplexed. The person kept offering me tea, coffee, or water as I continued to wait. Finally, at last, someone did come out. The person appeared to be in her early twenties and seemed to be confused but decided to walk me to a conference room and asked me to wait there. After twenty minutes, two other individuals came in to introduce themselves. Both stated that they were excited to have me there, to contribute to creating a better place for youngsters in the community. One was a director of a program but was not the one that I was placed with. The other was a licensed clinical social worker (LCSW) who worked in the agency's behavioral health program, which was also not where I was placed. Both individuals gave me different materials to read, and both assured me that the materials would take several hours. By this time, it was already noon, and the young person returned to the conference room and stated that I could take lunch. The person also said that I was on my own for lunch and that I had one hour.

I smiled and did not want to respond to the fact that I was a volunteer and an intern. But most importantly, I was an adult who probably was familiar with how work worked. I returned in exactly one hour, and the person was waiting in the lobby and handed me a schedule for the rest of the year. I reviewed the schedule, and it had exact time for breaks and lunches. In it was also a bathroom usage schedule. This was the first time that I'd seen a schedule of when I could use the bathroom. I wanted to ask my bladder if this was acceptable. It could not tell me, but I was sure that my bladder would disagree with the person's bathroom schedule.

The clinical supervisor who introduced herself and provided training prior to the placement did not work for the agency. She never revealed this information. In fact, she worked for a school district about three cities away from this agency and was moonlighting as a consultant for this agency. This information was later revealed to me after I tried to seek consultation and could not find the person in the agency's directory. My initial impression of this person was someone who was professional and competent. There was not any indication of the person's role other than a professional who was with the agency for a very long time. So, any contact was mostly done on the phone. Since I had no other experience dealing with a clinical supervisor before, I could not make a comparison to what an acceptable clinical supervisor's role was.

The second day was a little better. I was ushered to a cubicle, and it was dark in the area and the cubicle appeared to be a designation for storage of who knew what. There was a small empty area with a computer. The rest of the space in the cubicle was taken by boxes, documents, party favors, health prevention slogans, health flyers, program books, agency manuals, and brochures of all kinds from various places. I was handed a box of documents and told that in order to understand the agency, I needed to be involved in data entry. It was not the person's fault that this message was conveyed to me; however, I had spent more than twenty years conducting research studies and such an explanation did not jive with me. I remained silent and offered to open the box and inspect the surveys. It was interesting to examine the data. With my ego intact, I was convinced that they wanted me to analyze the data until the person came and instructed me to start data entry, and I could get help if I needed to know how to use SSPS (Statistical Programming for Social Scientists). I didn't.

I spent the first week entering data and tried to stick to the bathroom schedule by limiting caffeine intake and drinking water. I took lunch and breaks at the exact times on the schedule to avoid complications. By the end of the week, on Friday, a guy brought in three more boxes. They were giant, two times bigger than the box that took me the entire week to completely enter.

The first year of internship in this particular MSW program required a student to complete sixteen hours per week for the entire academic year. I scheduled my internship days on Tuesday and Thursday. By the second day of the second week, I realized, after calculating how long it would take me to enter each box that I would not escape this task. It would take me the entire internship time to complete data entry. I wanted to make sure that my tasks were not limited to data entry and that I could perform other tasks, such as seeing clients and conducting outreach or case management. So, this young person, whom I was told the first day would be my day-to-day manager, stated that if I wanted to help pass out flyers and documents, I should come in on Saturdays to meet parents and their children. The person also stated that these families were monolingual. They only spoke Spanish, and I do not speak Spanish. I could help out with cleaning the area at the end of the day. In fact, this person stated that all services in this particular program took place only on Saturdays. So, I asked to switch one of my weekdays to one Saturday per week, but I was told it would be unacceptable since it would take time away from data entry and that Saturdays would be an addition. I called the clinical supervisor and asked a series of questions concerning requirements dictated by the MSW department in terms of a type of field experience that I needed as a first-year student to gain foundation year knowledge and practice. The clinical supervisor used my first name repeatedly, in fact every other word. I was not sure if the person was trying to intimidate me or annoy me. I finally said, "I have in my records from you that I will be doing case management, and where is that in my internship, considering that services were provided on Saturdays to monolingual Spanish speakers?"

The clinical supervisor went silent for a few seconds before responding to my question. She finally said, "Your definition of case management is too strict."

I remember saying, "Please explain to me, so that I can have clarity on it."

The clinical supervisor rambled and ranted in a condescending tone for about an hour. At times, the person was scolding and yelling on the phone, "Suck it up, you're an intern." During the person's monologue, I remained silent until it got toward the end of the person's remarks. The clinical supervisor finally defined it as, "Anything can be case management, including data entry."

I responded by stating, "I am uncertain about your definition because it does not have human contact, face to face sometimes, you know like talking to people and helping them out with addressing their needs." I thanked the clinical supervisor for the definition and decided that Tuesday would be my last day at this agency. In the meantime, I followed up on the VA internship by sending a follow-up email to ask for an update. I'd had my second interview but had not heard back from them. The VA coordinator asked if I could start the following week and asked for available days in the week. But it was one month into the quarter. I was far too behind in hours since I would not get any from the first agency; however, I knew that I would get enough time since the VA required me to be there three days per week. I just needed 480 hours for the entire academic year and a pass of the final evaluation from the field instructor.

I was confused that day when I left the agency and sent out an email stating that it was going to be my last day at the end of the day. I was happy that my first oppression of being an intern had finally come to an end and I felt liberated. I was also nervous and worried about the new prospect of getting lost in a big system. I was also concerned about the commute hours, not in terms of distance but time due to bad traffic over the bridge and in the city. I had enjoyed the privilege of not having to get up early, and now I had to force myself to start waking up in the wee hours to get dressed and leave the house. I also did not want to take public transportation, but I'd have to. Driving to the city would be too stressful.

I was dropped off at the Bay Area Transit (BART) station the first day and took the train to the city center and waited for the VA bus to take me to the VA facility. The VA bus was not always on time. I was an hour or two late on a regular basis. By the end of the second week, I was growing tired and tried to supplement with private transportation. This took me about forty minutes to over an hour. My commute times averaged about two to three hours daily. I was getting tired by the end of the fall quarter and was not looking forward to returning in the winter and spring quarters, but I had run out of options and time. The winter quarter and internship was not an exciting time for me because I had to spend longer hours. I did try to keep a positive outlook with the VA experience. The field instructor didn't have any experience coaching and supervising interns. This clinical supervisor pretty much left us (me and the other intern) alone to do what we felt appropriate with our caseloads. I had a small caseload, and I also facilitated an anger management class with the field instructor. That went well until the Interpersonal Therapy (IPT) training started, and one of the seminar leaders viewed interns as nothing more than ignorant students who needed to be talked down to, disregarding our previous professional careers. The person started preaching and calling a group of us ungrateful for the opportunity when we checked our phones. I certainly had to check my phone regularly since my son was small and he was in a daycare program for the first time whereas prior to this, he was never far from me and had never spent time with a stranger. My worries were beyond the seminar and the internship. This person did not care. I dropped out toward the end of the training, not because of my experience with this person but because the one client I had to practice this theoretical orientation with left the bay area, and it was too late to recruit a new client with only two sessions left. The ITP approach needed 16 sessions to complete the entire training with multiple stages (initial, mid, and final stages) of intervention. The initial stage involved building rapport/therapeutic alliance and conducting an inventory (identifying support systems). I was told by the seminar leaders that IPT was known to treat depression effectively and was endorsed by the VA alongside CBT (Cognitive Behavioral Therapy). Not many known theoretical orientations were endorsed by the VA except various variations of exposure therapy (ET) and CBT.

Exposure therapy comprises several variations. According to the American Psychological Association website, ET is a psychological treatment that was developed to help people confront their fears. When people are fearful of something, they tend to avoid the feared objects, activities, or situations. ET has been known to be effective in the treatment or treatment component for fears and phobias, including:[i]

- Phobias
- Panic disorder
- Social anxiety disorder
- Obsessive-compulsive disorder
- Posttraumatic stress disorder
- Generalized stress disorder

There are many strategies used in ET. Specific examples include:

- **In vivo exposure**: The approach of this ET is to confront the fear head on. A person is asked to face a feared object, situation, or activity directly. For example, someone with a fear of snakes might be instructed to handle a snake, or someone with social anxiety might be instructed to give a speech in front of an audience.

- **Imaginal exposure:** In this modality, the idea is to discuss the feared object, situation, or activity deliberately through vivid imagination. For example, someone with posttraumatic stress disorder might be asked to recall and describe their traumatic experience in order to reduce feelings of fear.

- **Virtual reality exposure:** In some cases, virtual reality technology can be used when in vivo exposure is not practical. For example, someone with a fear of driving might drive a virtual car in the therapist's office, using equipment that provides the sights, sounds, and smells of a car.

- **Interoceptive exposure:** This intervention strives to deliberately bring on physical sensations that are harmless but fearful to the client. For example, someone with panic disorder might be instructed to run around in a small, confined and safe place in order to make his or her heart speed up and therefore feel that the sensation is not dangerous.

For more detailed information, it is best to visit the APA website. I just wanted to provide a brief overview of ET. In addition, ET can be introduced in multiple small doses or in different stages (time periods) and paces: [1]

- **Graded exposure**: The clinician helps the client construct an exposure fear hierarchy, in which feared objects, activities, or situations are ranked according to difficulty. They begin with mildly or moderately difficult exposures, and then progress to harder ones.

- **Flooding**: Using the exposure fear hierarchy to begin exposure with the most difficult tasks.

- **Systematic desensitization**: In some cases, exposure can be combined with relaxation exercises to make them feel more manageable and to associate the feared objects, activities, or situations with relaxation.

- **Emotional processing**: During exposure, the client can learn to attach new, more realistic beliefs to feared objects, activities, or situations, and can become more comfortable with the experience of fear.

Exposure therapy is thought to help a person in various aspects of their life. Some of these are:

> **Habituation**: Over time, people find that their reactions to feared objects or situations decrease.

> **Extinction**: Exposure can help weaken previously learned associations between feared objects, activities or situations and bad outcomes.

> **Self-efficacy**: Exposure can help show the client that they are capable of confronting their fears and can manage the feelings of anxiety.

Some other interventions that are highlighted here are those related to addiction treatments. One known intervention called "Seeking Safety" is known to be effective for the treatment of addiction and trauma. It was endorsed by and used in some local government agencies, but it was rejected by the VA. The proponents of the method pointed to research studies that proved their evidence-based practice. The Seeking Safety model is a present-focused (first stage) for addiction and trauma. The website Treatment Innovations has information about this model.ii Two treatment models that are recognized to have evidence-based outcomes and are accepted by larger institutions such as the federal government are Dialectical Behavioral Therapy (DBT) and Enhanced Motivational Interviewing Technique or Motivational Interviewing (MI). I did sign up for MI training, and it was a little easier. The facilitators were easygoing and seemed friendly. Both were new to the VA and young. Both seemed to understand that interns were not young and inexperienced and that they had other worries and obligations. I missed one session of the training but did the assignment. This was on Motivational Interviewing (MI) enhancement technique. One of the facilitators did provide a client to practice this technique on, and I was grateful. By this time, it was toward the end of the internship and I had already secured my next academic year internship. I mentally checked out by the end of March of that year even though I was physically present at the VA facility. Overall, it was a very memorable year and an interesting experience.

After the VA experience, I was looking for a specific type of field instructor. I was more intentional and deliberate in choosing a field instructor and an agency. This time, though, I did not want an inexperienced clinical supervisor or a paid (small as it might have been) internship due to expectations from the employer. I was seeking someone who had experience dealing with interns (foundation or advanced year students).

This was important at the time because I truly believed that the advanced year experience would determine a career path in social work for me.

Big systems are not for everyone. This was my biggest takeaway at the time. The training program was relatively good; however, the potential knowledge and experience from such a program rested heavily on the field instructor. If you have a bad one, you may experience an unpleasant or immemorable experience. If you get a good one, the experience tends to determine your career path as a social worker.

Smaller and experienced field instructors know what to do with interns and how to respond to their expectations. My rewards came late, but they came. I was hooked and felt for the first time that I was in a nurturing environment and valued for my work, unlike my experience with the VA. I felt burnt out and undervalued after I left the VA, but this was not the case at my second placement, largely due to the field instructor's training but most importantly because she treated her interns with mutual respect and patience.

Year 2 Part-time Internship

By the time I started the advanced year with my internship, I had few expectations but was happy to have shorter days and be able to work with children from TK to 6th grade. I was embarking on a journey with play therapy. It was a huge shift in mental capacity. I carried a small caseload at the VA facility, a lot smaller than at a public unified school district. But I was happy to be able to help children. They were challenging in many ways, however, they also made an impression on me. There was this sense of innocence that one discovered in children as opposed to adults who lived their lives and experienced things that no human being should. My curiosity got the best of me when it came to play therapy. I was familiar with CBT, IPT, DBT, and other theoretical orientations and models, but definitely not play therapy.

Children experience distinct social, cognitive, and emotional developmental changes between the ages of 6 and 12. Play therapy is defined as a "dynamic interpersonal relationship between a child (or person of any age) and a therapist trained in play therapy procedures who provides selected play materials and facilitates the development of a safe relationship for the child (or person of any age) to fully express and explore self (feelings, thoughts, experiences, and behaviors) through play, the child's natural medium of communication, for optimal growth and development."[iii] Play and art therapy seemed simple enough to utilize to help children in dealing with their challenges and addressing their development.

I started the internship a week before the fall quarter started, but then I realized that I could not bank the hours and was able to take off the last week before the two-week winter recess to catch up on school assignments. I had a caseload of 12 students ranging in ages from 6 years old to about 9 years old. My first two cases involved two second graders from the same ethnic origin as myself; one had an uncle, and the other girl's parents were killed in a traffic collision. Both were in shock. And it turned out that the father who was killed was not the girl's biological father. Her biological father was still alive and was living in Texas. In fact, upon research, I discovered that the man and his girlfriend (the little girl's mother) had been caring for both his mother and the little girl since she'd been a toddler. She did not know and was not made aware of her own biological father until the couple's death.

There were more discoveries about this family and the connection to my past. In fact, the little girl whose uncle was killed turned out to be the daughter of one of my clients I worked with as a youth counselor for a nonprofit agency twenty years prior. I had the opportunity to provide counseling and connect with her mother, who was my formal client. The formal client had a job at Kaiser as a receptionist. She married her middle school sweetheart who worked as an auto mechanic. This formal client was referred to me for being sexually active and was pregnant at the age of twelve years old. This pregnancy was her oldest child who was at the same age when I was her counselor (I was twenty-something then), and who was about to turn twenty-one years old. The prediction from some of the service providers then was that this formal client would not graduate from high school and would not remain with the same boy.

One other case that stood out for me was a six-year-old boy who liked to steal things from his teacher's desk. He would take pens, books, candies, papers, and anything he could get his hands on. It was with this student that I understood how to use sand tray play therapy. Sand tray play therapy with non-directive approach is a way for children to express their experiences and feelings through a natural, self-guided, self-healing process. Children often communicate through play about their past or present experiences, and sand tray play becomes an important vehicle for them to know and accept themselves and others, according to the Court Appointed Special Advocates for Children.[iv] Through sand tray play therapy, this first grader began talking about his family while playing with tool soldiers in the sand. I discovered that he was homeless, had been living in a car for about three months, and was eating cereal for breakfast, lunch, and dinner. He then moved in with his paternal grandmother and lived with her until his mother returned a year later. His father was absent for most of his life, but when he showed up, he would give this first grader unwanted gifts like pens, pencils, and paper. His father would turn to face his mother and they would yell at each other. So, the teacher's desk was a reminder of a father who yelled at his mother. The desk was a trigger for him. Two months into the school year, his family moved to another city about an hour away, and he was taken out of school without any notice.

I participated in the COST (Coordination of Services Team) meetings occasionally but not consistently. I did not know people at the COST meeting, and they did not seem to care if I attended or not. Besides, it was late in the afternoon and was difficult to pick up my son and be at the meetings at the same time. It was difficult to maintain my presence when I had other obligations. I tried to be more consistent during the last three months of my internship. I did learn a few things about the process of COST. Most COST meetings that I attended focused heavily on truancy instead of other behavioral issues (e.g., trauma-related issues, ADHD, anger control, depression, anxiety, etc.). My post-MSW degree COST meetings were a little different due to my role and responsibilities as a behavioral health program manager. I felt that I was taken more seriously as a post-MSW degree social worker. Perhaps because I was working where the principal was female as opposed to the first school, where the principal was a white male and busy trying to save his job. Prior to my internship, he was almost forced out by some teachers.

Lessons Learned

Knowing exactly what to do can save time and headaches. It is difficult to choose the internship that is right because what is right depends on needs and interests. I know that the experience that I will gain will be determined only by comparison to my past professional experience. The VA is a big system, and it can be difficult to navigate, even with the experience and knowing the right people. While I was in the loop in terms of office politics, from what I gathered by listening to staff there, the VA system is complex and complicated. Office politics in the context of a big system such as the VA appeared to be about power and control, which some people saw as a stepping stone to promotions and better job mobility within the system. I steered clear, with an out of sight and out of mind approach, to keep myself invisible and did not feel the need to even secure references at the time. I had a good reason. I did not want to work for that facility and did not think that I would return to work for the VA anytime soon. My takeaways from the VA are as follows:

- Large systems, such as the VA, are tricky. I think one needs to be politically and socially savvy to engage in a complex system successfully. The energy and effort to invest in office politics may be a huge price to pay for those who are like me. I could not juggle my personal life, real job, schoolwork, and internship. I preferred to stay under the radar, knowing that I would never return to such a place.

- Large systems need a person who is politically savvy and enjoys engaging in office politics and power plays. I think that for most of us, we see it as stupidity and something that is not worth time or energy unless you enjoy self-torture. And I view office politics as disproportionate stupidity.

- One thing about a large system is that there is not much of a worry for funding since it is generally secured. Therefore, the job is relatively secure, but that comes with a cost. Imagine a working bee. In a big system, each staff is more like a robot or working bee who accepts the role and recognizes the importance of that role. No cowboy-like behaviors or taking creative steps are allowed. A big system is rigid. Change is slow.

It is important to understand that the experience from an internship or placement, whether great or small, is heavily contingent on the field instructor.

Conclusion

This chapter focused on the introduction to field placements. I discussed personal experiences and offered insight into the world of both small and large systems. I discussed the different approaches that may be significant in gaining experiences as an intern, including tips and hints on what mattered most when choosing a placement.

The next chapter focuses on the methodology used to guide this ethnography. I discuss various methods, including participant-observation, informal dialogues, and group sharing. While this project is not a research study, some elements of research study were used, such as keeping notes with dates and topics, organizing by major themes, and adhering to confidentiality practices.

CHAPTER 2

Ethnographic Fieldwork

I am at a crossroad between social work and anthropology. Before I was a social worker, I was an anthropologist. It seemed natural to borrow a methodology from one field to understand another. While generally I am an anthropologist, I chose to study my "own" community that is the social-work-student community and focused on social work experience as a community. I have always been both an insider and an outsider as an anthropologist who studied her "own culture." As you can see, I put these phrases in quotation marks. I left Cambodia when I was very young and returned many decades later to study a community there. I felt equally like an outsider, as I did an insider. These conflicting identities created a unique opportunity for me to see certain things differently than those that considered themselves to be either one or the other.

My MSW degree took me almost four years to complete. I was first enrolled in the full-time program and then had to reapply to the part-time program. After enrolling in the part-time program, I learned one difficult and annoying problem. I could not transfer all the units from the full-time program to the part-time program because they were placed in a different department. I did not question the program director whether all units would be transferrable at the time. In hindsight, I would ask this question as it involves time and money. And it also increased the stress and pressure of passing a course. The explanation for the reason of limited transferable units was that it was housed in a different department. The part-time program was a self-supporting type of program without the support of public funding, in contrast to the full-time program that is supported by state funds. This part-time program, unable to sustain itself or renew its credential, ended two years after I graduated. During the four years I was part of both programs, I learned a great deal about academics' interactions, students' lives, and struggles. My smallest class size was twenty and the largest was thirty. I had four classes initially (in the full-time program). So, on average, I encountered sixty people per quarter. I took courses during the summer as well. So, this was a total of at least one hundred and eighty people, give or take. Although most of my encounters with them were in a classroom setting, I did learn a few things between breaks and during various department activities beyond traditional pedagogy or formal instruction. The size was representative of a small village or community with specific activities (learning, engaging in group assignments, and absorbing what was presented).

Ethnographic fieldwork is defined as a methodology used by anthropologists to collect data to understand and seek explanations as well as interpretations of human behavior, beliefs, practices, and values. My version of conducting an ethnography goes beyond studying a group of people and their culture in a foreign country, such as a village with specific economic activities; rather, I focused on a group of people that shared some common practices on how to obtain in-depth skills in a particular career field. The traditional ethnography tends to focus on studying a culture or an ethnic community about their beliefs, values, practices, and lifeways. Ethnographic methods encompass a wide range of research methods, including surveys, face-to-face interviews, casual conversations, as well as field observations. A key methodology that is commonly used is participant observation. I was a participant in an MSW program and an observer who studied it.

Ethnography: What is it?

I define ethnography as a written picture of a group of people or a community that describes lifeways, cultural beliefs, and practices. It tells a story of a group of people that have certain commonalities about the way they live, work, play, and worship, generally. In addition, we should now include how they use or don't use technology since the inventions of smartphones and other smart devices that influence our daily lives.

Field Observations

As an anthropologist, it is difficult for me not to observe what is going on in the field or in a community in front of me. In this context, this was my community. It was the MSW students' community, and they were my cohorts. I spent three years with them and saw some of the most interesting dynamics emerge when one was confronted with competing tasks: school, work, and family. Beside exhaustion that sometimes could take a toll on all of us, the departmental politics and interpersonal dynamics further added pressure to this group of people. Work itself was, and is, stressful. Most students in the MSW program also had full-time jobs either in the field or in a related field. This combined juggling created a lot of stress that pushed students with even the smallest negative encounters or obstacles. This community, however, is not unique. As an insider, I could relate to their experiences and learned what worked for some and did not work for others. Because I had always been a part of academia, I never felt that I was far away from learning. Some of the students struggled quite a bit to pass classes and to function in a school environment. Three things that are worth highlighting regarding being a student in the MSW program:

- Making friends early in the program can help with building a support system beyond family.

- Get to know faculty and begin building a relationship with some of them, so they can write a letter of recommendation tailoring the specific skills and strengths that would stand out among many other students that professors write letters for.

- Develop networks in the field with colleagues who are already in the field practicing.

Making friends seems easy for some, but it can be extremely difficult. I encountered some difficulties given that I did not have the time or the energy or the right skills to make friends. I was never into making friends. I prefer to study people and how they interact with one another and the dynamics that emerge as a result. This was more interesting to me than living the experience. This was my struggle at the same time. The problem with not making friends was that I had to interact with classmates for about four years while I was in the program. The two cohorts proved to be resourceful for jobs and other opportunities. So, getting to know them while I was in the program was, and is, an advantage. Since my future was in academia, I knew that I needed to get myself reacquainted with some of the professors. At the time, it was more important for me to make sure that they knew who I was on a personal level, not just my academic performance or professional experience by being in the program. I was convinced, and still am, that professors can provide unique perspectives for students. I believe it is important to be unique, beyond just being outstanding. I started early building networks with professionals who were already practicing because I knew that I wanted to understand what this new career was all about as much as I could before heading down that career path for the rest of my life. I was in my mid-40s and I did not think that I had that many options to start something new and heavy, but perhaps something for fun that required less time and money. My goal then was to ask some of them to write letters of recommendation, but in the end, I could not get even one professor to write for me. One claimed that one semester was too limited a time to write anything meaningful.

Out of these three areas, I failed miserably in making friends. I kept in contact with three of the people in my cohort on a regular basis. I did not bother to try to keep in touch with the others. I attributed this to my character flaws. I generally do not like to interact with people because I prefer to study them. You can blame the field of anthropology for this character flaw if you want. My interests in learning about people's lives led me to socialize less with people and observe more about the interactions that people have with one another. As an anthropologist who studied her "own culture," I felt like an outsider. My rationale then was that I had been away from the country for over twenty years and hardly anything was familiar to me anymore. I used the same rationale when I was an MSW student. I was in it along with everyone else who had never taken graduate level courses in social work. I felt the same way with this small group of people who were about to embark collectively on this journey to the future with the aim of keeping in mind one oath in the field of social work with the ideals of engaging in social justice activism. I was proud to be a part of the group but on the periphery. I thought it kept me sane. I still think this is true. By keeping my distance, I was less involved in the drama that tends to come with group dynamics.

Reflexivity in Qualitative Research

As an anthropologist and now a social worker, I often wonder about how the findings will be used in academia and other places or the usefulness of reflexivity in qualitative research. Over the course of twenty years of conducting research studies and experience in the field and various ethnic communities, I have learned the importance of a researcher's knowledge of the culture, community settings, historical context, and environment of a study. Such insight into the lives of participants can greatly contribute to the richness of research findings. The concept of reflexivity as discussed by D'Cruz et al.[v] validates the importance of studying others and recognizes how our own lens as researchers influence or inform the research findings. D'Cruz et al. state that reflexivity has become more important in social work literature as it relates to social work education. This seems to be the case with my own experience as an anthropologist, researcher, and now a social worker who conducts research studies in a community setting.

My work thus far has involved reflexivity because of its 20/20 hindsight that allows a researcher/writer to understand the complexity and dynamics of human interactions to emerge, including daily problems encountered living in a complex and modern world. I was able to see things more objectively and was able to analyze problems in a more succinct and solid way once I lived past the experience and looked back on it. I have never tried to write notes when I was in a field situation. Although subjective experience offers great insight into human interactions and problem-solving, I believe that looking back at a situation with minimal documentation during the time provides us more clarity and objectivity. It is for this reason that I used reflexivity in my own research.

Limitations

This ethnography is limited in time and scope. Observations were conducted during my time taking MSW classes and the two years in a post-MSW program. There were neither formal interviews nor surveys to explore possible and pertinent questions concerning students' views on their experiences. This ethnography is purely observational and an insider's experiences interacting with varied people. This is not meant to be scientific and objective like a research study; therefore data was not designed to be collected in that scientific manner. I was one of the members, and we had relationships, including social interactions outside of the MSW program. Because this was not a research study, I only observed group dynamics in various stages of bonding. I interacted only with some of them and listened to their complaints whenever offered, but no probing was involved to elicit any further information than what was shared with me. In addition, the handwritten or typed notes were meant for my own recollection in case I was to write this ethnography.

Conclusion

This chapter focused on methodology used to collect information for the purpose of writing this ethnography. I focused on two key concepts of data collection. One is called participant-observation, a methodology that is used in the field of anthropology. The second method is referred to as reflexivity. This method is useful to analyze qualitative data and offers rich context into lives from the perspective of the observer.

The next chapter focuses on the nitty-gritty aspects of being a social worker. I will discuss different aspects of social work training, starting with case presentations, trauma, and things that trigger. I will discuss and describe these different areas of training and their importance, whether the social work degree is right for those who wish to pursue it and what personality needs to ensure success in the field. It is a long and difficult investment. The journey is not always easy, so choosing the right degree can propel an individual to have a long and meaningful career. I will discuss the ins and outs of being in a social program and compare that experience with those of other academic training programs.

CHAPTER 3

Case Presentations, Vicarious trauma, and Things That Trigger

Introduction

Case presentations, vicarious trauma, and things that trigger are something that I wished I learned more in-depth when I was in the program before I started my career as a social worker. I was getting some training, but I feel it was a passing mention as something to look for and consider. This chapter will focus on these key issues.

Each topic has its own value in social work practice. The classes themselves did not address case presentations. I learned how to conduct case presentations effectively through the VA field placements in a way that I believe would have been useful. In other words, it lacked the link from classroom to field, or the gap between training and internship that should have been filled. Similarly, the topic of various traumas was briefly but never fully introduced in a way that was thoughtful and systemic. In other words, there should have been an emphasis on the importance of how vicarious trauma plays in the perpetuation of introducing more trauma in work settings for social workers. Finally, it would be useful to have basic training on things that trigger. In this chapter, I will discuss these three issues in depth because I believe they are important to avoid burnout.

Case Presentations

My first case involved a male African American patient at a nursing home. He appeared to have some developmental disabilities with child-like demeanor and about a second-grade level of comprehension. He was a very friendly man who liked to talk about his past experiences when his family was still together. He was in his late 60s when I met him. The second case involved another male African American, this one a veteran who was deployed to Vietnam. He was diagnosed with PTSD and psychosis. He appeared to have developmental disabilities as well but they were very subtle. He was extremely nice and open. He was energetic and seemed to always be in a good mood except when a voice demanded him to end his life. By the third case, I concluded that all those in my caseload during the three years merged into one big mountain of stories connected to unfamiliar faces and yet were with very familiar faces. The importance of gaining experience in case presentations only became clear after I graduated from the program. I can now talk loosely about cases without realizing that I was conducting a case presentation.

What is case presentation? It could be loosely defined as telling a story of a person or it could be structured as a presentation in a classroom, depending on a class instructor's or field instructor's method of delivery of information. Some of them demanded some kind of structure that included identifying information, presenting problems, and intervention. Others preferred more detailed information, including identifying information, history of the person/family, other biopsychosocial information, case formulation, intervention, and case summary. The basic case formula includes:

- Identifying information,
- Context of the case (history/environment/family),
- Presenting problem(s), and
- Treatment plan.

Repetitiveness works. I know that if something is repeated often enough, it will naturally come to me as if I do not have to think about it. This is the case with me after eighteen months post-MSW degree because I do not know how many times per day that I had to summarize a case. Sometimes, I presented more than five times to more than five people. Case presentation is easy. I got it!

What is different in terms of how to present a case effectively depends on the level of training and maturity. I suppose one could turn to cognitive processes and the variability from one person to another. For example, one's background will heavily influence one's view of the case. There is no way of getting around personal biases. Being agnostic such as me does not provide a more objective lens as I am also influenced by my own surroundings, cultural values, and educational experience. So, it is important to be intentional about personal bias or become aware of oneself when working with people. It seems at times easier for me being an anthropologist as my professional training and experience allow me to reflect and contemplate on both positions as both an insider and outsider. It is also confusing since I can wear multiple hats now as an anthropologist, a social worker, an advocate, a researcher, and a teacher.

There is nothing like having bad experiences. These experiences stick in my head. They come to the forefront of my mental space when I least expect. Below, I outline case presentations to give in-depth understanding of how or when I think I got it.

Case Presentation Outline

If I stated that I tried too hard to learn about the art of case presentation, it would be an understatement. In the age of googling and instant research gratification, I did just that and even bought several books to learn how to present. At this time in my career, I had been a faculty for quite some time and was used to making presentations and giving lectures, including teaching various classes. However, I could not help myself but jot down important key points to put in the case presentation. Some of the things that are important are as follows:

- Demographics: Age, gender, ethnicity, living situation, and a brief statement of your own involvement

- Key findings: Presenting problem(s) and reason for intervention

- Background: Historical causes to give context

- Formulation: Provide reasons that led to presenting the problem(s)

- Interventions and plans: Describe what you have done and what you still plan to do about presenting the problem(s)

- Reason for your case presentation: Why you choose to present this case:

    o Is this an unusual case that poses challenges to an existing treatment model or approach of intervention?

    o Does it demonstrate the effectiveness of an intervention?

    o Do you need help identifying some of the challenges and solutions in this case?

    o Do you want to share your experiences or lessons learned?

Case presentations came easier once I got to practice frequently. These outlines and questions come naturally to me when I think of a case that challenges me psychologically, emotionally, and intellectually. I will live, breathe, and think about it until I've exhausted all options. For me, complicated cases do not necessarily imply big problems that are serious or life-threatening (unthinkable for anyone to commit) but just that they are different than what I have experienced before. I had no way of knowing how to develop an intervention prior to the MSW training. In fact, some of the more severe and unthinkable cases can be easier than those that are strange in nature. One comes to mind, but this was post-MSW program and involved extreme sensitivity.

I am referring to a borderline personality disorder diagnosis, but too young to be officially diagnosed as such.

Case Presentation Example

One of the more interesting cases that I was involved in was that of an elderly man who lived at a nursing facility at the time when I met him and eventually was included in my caseload. He was somewhat developmentally delayed but was a very nice, gentle man. He was friendly and articulative in an almost innocent, child-like manner. It took me three months to learn that he had no one left to care for him. His daughter had died while he was hospitalized five years earlier. His wife also died many years before that. He was the only child and grew up almost all alone when his parents died in his early twenties. At first impression, I could not tell why someone who had no one left to care for seemed so happy about life and friendly toward others. I was a stranger then and was new to the field of social work. My only experience in this area was the kind of life I had lived and the experiences attached to me from being in war and living under an oppressive communist regime when I was a little girl.

He was the second client that stood out for me, and I presented to the class simply because he was different from all the others. During my training, some workshops on stress and anxiety management encouraged steering oneself away from negative behaviors and negative people. This experience led me to believe part of his longevity stemmed from his positive outlook on life.

He was in a nursing home and his only window to the outside world was paid professionals like me, although I was only an intern and did not get paid to provide services to him. I was still a part of the professional team that came to visit and provide him services. So, he took it with great stride, grace, and ease. Beside the fact that he was a lot older than most nursing home residents, there was nothing else that stood out to me. He seemed healthy beside the fact that he was struggling with several health problems related to aging. We went for walks regularly, and I usually spent more time with him than the other five clients who lived at the nursing home. I did enjoy myself and kept wondering if social work was about being social and cordial to a lonely senior in a nursing home. By the third meeting, I learned he'd spent some years in jail, and no one ever came to visit him while he was incarcerated. He stated his mother was always busy, but he could not tell whether she was working or just being busy with life. His father was absent for most of his life and barely knew him. He made friends the years he was incarcerated, but he outlived them all. He was proud to be living alone with his life without regrets. He did not want children or to get married. He said he did not want the responsibilities of being a parent. His analysis of his own experiences growing up in poor urban America was that things were generally normal but with a few major challenges that tested his own values as an African American male, considering he grew up in the 1950s and 1960s. In many ways, the civil rights movement created an impression on him that spoke to the struggles during that time with racism, discrimination, injustice, and poverty. He said he did not want to rear children and have them exposed to those unpleasant experiences.

Like any case presentation that I had to present to a group of people, this one was no different. I started with identifying information, a summary of challenges, case formulation, and case context, and ended with a treatment plan. Unlike any case that I presented in the MSW program in the past, I did not have anything unique about the case to present that would offer compelling or complicated discussion for the group. There was nothing new to learn from this case. I wanted to present because he was different. He was aging, sick, and alone. He had no children. He had no family members or friends left. They had all passed away. He was positive about life despite the fact he could not walk and could barely breathe. He was positive. This was a unique perspective on life. It was the first time that I presented a case without much in the way of anything new to learn about a human being. I simply wanted to present a case that involved someone who loved to live life the way he knew how despite all his challenges. I was his case manager for four months, and he never complained a single time about his life or the challenges that he was dealing with. Toward the end of my internship, he had a place that he could move into before his nursing stay expired.

Case Presentation Example 2

The second case presentation was a veteran of Afghanistan. He was in his early thirties and was unemployed. He tried to get an approval for service connection and was going through some difficulties with the VA system such as filing the wrong forms, talking to the wrong people, and being late in responding to claims. He lost his condo when he lost his job. His girlfriend broke up with him when he could not manage his own symptoms. Service connection is the equivalence of disability, but it is for veterans. The process of obtaining an approval appeared to be a mystery since criteria were never fully disclosed or made known by the committees that review cases. However, there is extensive work involved in the application, and it takes time to get a veteran to get connected to services. Service connection means support services that include financial compensation. For some veterans, this financial compensation is their livelihood. It comes with monthly financial payments, and it is like social security paychecks. Also, service connection may provide health insurance with full pay for all services related to medical needs if they are approved 100% (most receive some percentage below 100%). I believe veterans pay for some portions whenever they seek services. I am uncertain how it works precisely. My knowledge stems from listening to veterans' stories. My role was limited to hearing all their grievances against the government and community.

His case was complicated. His lack of interest in people and building skills to better himself was an example. He talked about how no one could understand the hardship and violence he witnessed in theater (war zone) and no one cared about his struggles. I listened to him and it seemed to be enough for him. I could not say exactly what I had done for him except to open my heart and ears to learn about his experiences. On the outside, he seemed fine. There was not a physical scar that was obvious to me. We had five sessions and then he moved to a northern California veterans' home.

This second case presentation was different. I did not follow the course instruction with all that data but rather I articulated, based on my own version of what I thought was important. It was to me about sharing his story, period.

The field liaison asked me after my case presentation what the case was about. I responded simply, "He's not a case." What matters in case presentation is what you deem important from the eye of your client. They will let you know what they want, not just need, to live fulfilling lives. Addressing the wants and needs as told by clients is key to capturing the essence of a case.

I did not get full points for this case presentation, but I felt liberated for telling his story. Is there a moral to the story for a case presentation? Yes, do what is right by you and your clients, not by a standard pedagogy. Speak from the heart. Try to feel what others feel about their lives. It is important to advocate for yourself and for your client, but do not burn down the house that you live in. This was, and is, my life mantra. It means push as hard as I can but retreat whenever I have no more energy to go on and save what is left to fight another day.

Vicarious Trauma

I did not realize the significance of knowing how to address vicarious trauma nor did I take it seriously when I was in the MSW program. Honestly, I did not think that it mattered much to be deliberately focused on the grieving process. I had attended several trainings on vicarious trauma, but somehow it was placed in the back of my mental space, and I did not put it as a priority for daily practice or incorporate it in my self-care practice. At the time when I started writing this ethnography, there were eighteen school shootings. It was barely through February. It was also interesting times with Donald Trump in the White House, and the Black Lives Matter and Me Too movements were in full swing. By the eighteenth school shooting, in Parkland, Florida, students from the high school were furious and demanded policy change. They started the Never Again movement. They were loud and they were clear. The politicians appeared to be caught off guard and stalled for time. The National Rifle Association (NRA) blamed the media for all the gun problems. The only suggestion from the White House was to have teachers carry guns.

I had limited training on vicarious (secondary) trauma while in the program. I did receive some after I graduated and worked in a school setting, but it was mostly related to the specific time and place or an incident such as a recent mass shooting. I remember attending a county quality improvement meeting, and some of the attendees requested to have vicarious trauma training. They wondered, like I did, what students were feeling and whether they were afraid to go to school. Vicarious trauma seemed to be at the forefront of this. At this time, I came to understand that I also needed to understand how this impacted me personally, not just the students who were served by mental health professionals. I had not thought much about the importance of self-care until I started diving deep into how trauma impacted our brain and what happened with repeated experiences of trauma. Yes, there is a thing called neuroplasticity.

Neuroplasticity looks like little fingers and they are the brain's neuronal connections. These neuronal connections, the little fingers, reduce in length with repeated trauma, but they are also adaptable. They can grow back given the right environment. Another way of looking at this is through the triune brain structures. The executive part of the brain, the prefrontal cortex, in a normal brain without exposure to trauma, operates in a 2 to 1 ratio, and the ratio is approximately 1 to 1 in a person with an experience of trauma. The part of the brain that is responsible for alerting dangers becomes more heightened with individuals who have experienced trauma. The brain areas that have shown to be implicated in the stress response are the amygdala, hippocampus, and prefrontal cortex.[vi] Traumatic stress can create lasting changes in these brain areas. The amygdala (the body's alarm circuit) is the integrative center for emotions, emotional behavior, and motivation.[vii] The hippocampus is in the inner region of the temporal lobe, which is part of the limbic system that is responsible for regulating emotional responses.[viii] It plays a major role in learning and memory. This structure is fragile and is easily damaged by external stimuli. It is associated with our long-term memory.[ix] The prefrontal cortex is responsible for executive functions.[x] It relates to our abilities to differentiate many thoughts that are conflicting, such as the ability for us to determine good or bad, better or best, and future consequences of current activities. We have evolved to have such a gift, but that gift comes with a price if we do not treat it right. In the case of vicarious trauma, we need a lot of processing and healing time to ensure that we do not pass such a scar down to the next generation.

I have my routine to combat this difficult part of the work as a social worker who encounters daily trauma. I have my morning tea, aromatherapy in the garden (I smell things in my own garden), and I water my herb and floral pots in the morning and in the afternoon when I get home. I light candles in the evenings and enjoy sipping coffee or wine in front of my yard whenever there is a nice day. Walking and strolling in the neighborhood helps with letting go of the day's traumatic experiences. I also discovered that contemplation and dreaming helps to ease the burden of a work life and create a space for balancing personal life and stressful work. Physical activities seem to work best with reducing symptoms of vicarious trauma. Walking, running, or dancing helps reduce stress and anxiety. If physical activities are your cup of tea, make them a part of your daily routine. Your body and mind will thank you later.

Things that Trigger

One never really knows for sure what events trigger emotional or psychological reactions that are detrimental to the health and well-being or impair one's ability to function either momentarily or long-term. However, there are a few factors that are worth highlighting. These include past experiences, one's own recognition of past experiences through direct or indirect associations, and specific negative emotions or feelings related to past events (including sounds, smell, or visual displays that may not have any association to the actual past event). I suppose our memory system is like a filing system and, nothing in it is gone, and everything in it, once filed, permanently remains. But unlike a file, one cannot just discard it when it is deemed not useful anymore. Experiences in our memory system cannot be physically thrown away, so this is when aspects of CBT may be useful and are effective in managing our reactions to past experiences. This is about manipulation of our thoughts, beliefs, and behaviors in a positive way by removing negative cognitions and installing positive ones. We can change the way we think and how we feel about these negative emotions by deliberately and consciously changing the beliefs about what happened or reframing our experiences in a way that is beneficial to our survivability. Some of the strategies that may prove effective are as follows:

- Throw away the guilt, the shame, or the regrets by focusing on replacing with good things, good memories, good food, good friends, or pleasurable cues in our lives.

- Allow time to heal. Know that it takes time and energy to constantly remind the brain (yourself) that it is not okay to travel back to the same event and ruminate past experiences and replay such thoughts/experiences over and over, keeping them in the forefront of the mental space. Maintain a present- or future-focused approach and set a reminder that this is what can be controlled. Realize that the past cannot be changed.

- Purge out rumination and racing thoughts by forcing the brain to think about something else that is meaningful and deserves to be in that mental space. Use attention of focus approach, which is to choose a phrase that is hard enough to remember and repeat over and over. This is to distract from racing thoughts.

Focusing on food that is good for the body and the brain is an example of a meaningful self-care practice. Banana, avocados, and berries are good for both the brain and body. The brain will release dopamine whenever it sees these goodies. I call it accessing your own natural high. The same goes for the brain. Feed it with nuts and greens. Nature walks and being close to a body of water helps with maintaining good mental health. A balanced self-care practice should include ensuring at least two hours per week of nature walks or being close to water.

I use the metaphor or a wild beast that needs constant taming to reference our brains. Put it on a leash and hold tight. When we let go of the brain, it can run loose down a rabbit hole. I am referring to racing or intrusive thoughts. The more negative experiences one has, the more likely one will develop some of these thoughts. Learn to manage them through meditation or thought-stopping techniques (telling oneself to stop thinking about these thoughts). One can train one's brain to think what one wants it to think. Learning to control one's own thoughts takes practice and becoming aware of when thoughts are flowing in and out. Choose to bring these thoughts back to the forefront of one's mental space and become critical of them. Three actions one can take are to:

- Ask yourself why you feel the way you feel.

- Ask yourself what to do with these thoughts.

- Dismiss or minimize these thoughts through forcing yourself to think of something else that is generally positive or meaningful for you.

Because we do not know what triggers us, it is important to begin building positive files to reduce the files of negative experiences. A solid self-care practice involves building up these positive experiences. Learning to know one's brain is a good start. Listen to one's own emotions. Know when it is time to seek help, support, or set aside "me time" to decompress, rejuvenate, and recompose.

Conclusion

This chapter discussed the applications of social work and how to manage our lives as we are immersed in this type of work. Social work is hard work but also rewarding. So, I find that it is important to find formulas that work, and there is no single strategy because what works for one person may not work for another. I have learned some important lessons by being in the MSW program. One example is on the value of case presentations. By knowing exactly what and how to convey ideas to people, I was already fulfilling the first step in the role of a social worker.

This chapter focused on case presentations and what to highlight in a client's life. I discussed the importance of learning by presenting in a classroom. I also discussed vicarious trauma and how to address symptoms even though they are absent from one's conscious mind. Finally, I briefly pointed out things that trigger and the importance of incorporating meaningful activities into one's life to have a good balance of personal life and work.

The next chapter focuses on minor technicalities. In the next chapter, I dive deep into the practice of good self-care and the issues related to working with clients and how their stories are interwoven with those who serve them. Specifically, I will discuss three areas: transference, countertransference, self-care practice for professionals, and other important factors in understanding our brains and the role of keeping a good balance between life and work.

CHAPTER 4

Minor Technicalities

Introduction

The best part about being a social worker is the stories that clients tell. The worst part about being a social worker is also the stories that clients tell when they come to ask for help. I enjoyed every single moment of my time with my clients. I also experienced nightmares and have triggers because of the stories they told me. This is called secondary or vicarious trauma. It is transmissible. What one is feeling is real. Clients' stories as a form of trauma are transmissible.

In this chapter, I will discuss some key areas of social work (mental health/clinical) practice: transference, counter-transference self-care practice for professionals, and other important factors in understanding our brains and the role of keeping a good balance between life and work.

Trauma is Transmissible!

(Negative) stories are a form of trauma, especially those that are violent and intense. Vicarious or secondary trauma is transmissible. This was first made apparent to me after I graduated from the MSW program. In fact, I'd already worked in the field of social work for almost two years. While I engaged in a lot of clinical practice to attempt to earn hours for licensing as a Licensed Clinical Social Worker (LCSW), I came across one story from a psychiatrist. By this time, the shift from research on the intersectionality of culture and health to trauma had begun. I was very focused on what happened when we witness or live through a violent event. This was from a purely selfish perspective. As a child, I lived through the Vietnam War and the Pol Pot regime. I felt it was time to work closer to home, figuratively speaking, by looking inward instead of outward. It was about how I was impacted by trauma from these regimes and what happened in my own brain. Those experiences became recurrent negative thoughts in my mind. Whenever I was under stress, they became active (racing) and overwhelmed my system (my mind and body). While searching articles in various newspapers, one article popped out and piqued my interest. It was a story in a newspaper article that described a psychiatrist who was experiencing symptoms of PTSD. The psychiatrist stated that he had never experienced trauma in his life, but his symptoms emerged when he started treating clients with traumatic experiences and those that had been diagnosed with PTSD. It was then, he realized that their stories had become his own experiences. The first study on trauma transmissibility was conducted with children of holocaust survivors.[xi] The study examined children of holocaust survivors who exhibited symptoms of PTSD, but they had never experienced any traumatic events in their lives. Why do our brains react this way to violence? My best understanding is that we are wired in our brains to capture dangers and create signals to warn us about future events. In many ways, our brains use these past experiences to predict future outcomes. While we know past actions may have the same outcomes as future actions, our reactions (event > belief > thoughts > future actions) whether at the conscious or subconscious, reflect on that exact past outcome. Therefore, we get anxious, worried, and our systems are overwhelmed by the same mistakes because our brains say so, not because we will make the same mistakes.

I believe one way of understanding this experience would be with friends, which I assume most of us have in our lifetime. Some friends we like, but some friends we wish we'd never met. It is this latter type that I am referencing, the kind that tend to unload their problems whenever they get a chance. These stories (problems) are a type of vicarious trauma. These negative experiences tend to get stored and replayed in our brains when we least expect. We, whether consciously or unconsciously, tend to run away from meeting these friends for fear that all they will talk about are those problems. Or we inadvertently complain to other friends about them and drag our feet to see them. How does one avoid such an opportunity to be unloaded upon? One effective strategy I find useful is to make plans with specific agendas or goals that are physical or involves a conversation subject besides dealing with personal problems. Some view friends as a form of support, but it is important to keep in mind that there is a mutual understanding of what this exchange should look like. I tend to think that I need to have positive experiences when spending time with friends.

Vicarious trauma seemed unreal during my internships when I was in the MSW program. It seemed to only affect my emotional well-being during the post-MSW degree and when I began working with young people in a well-known community that was impacted by street gang violence. Their (trauma) stories have integrated into my own trauma and stories. Having said this, I do have one disclaimer. I grew up in a war-torn country, lived through a war, and grew up in a ghetto that was also impacted by gun violence, drugs, and poverty while I was growing up in America. So, I cannot discount counter transference. I might have suffered more than the average social worker who probably grew up in a different community setting or a less violent environment.

Transference and Counter Transference

Counter transference as a concept seemed difficult to feel and identify. I did not understand it until the feelings impacted me while working as a social worker after the MSW program. These feelings were generally negative and affected me in many ways and often triggered me in a way that forced me to travel back to my past negative experiences. While I did not have many symptoms of PTSD, some emotional reactions (symptoms) tend to occur occasionally, such as nightmares or thoughts of past trauma because of triggering events. It became clearer once I was in the field on a more consistent basis. That is why self-care is an important safeguard against any negative impact from absorbing client stories.

On the other hand, transference seems easier to understand. It often refers to the emotional response of the client to the therapist.[xii] Some of these responses are positive and others can be negative. I had clients quit on me without knowing precisely why this happens. It is always a good idea to put initial reactions to the forefront of the discussion during the initial session to gauge the potential for any negative reactions and to evaluate if what you, as a social worker, are doing is working for the client. I often check in quickly to see if our goals (mine and the client's) are aligned. This means to have a responsible and sound practice as a mental health clinician. Therapy really is about focusing on an interpersonal process more than anything else. Building a positive relationship contributes greatly to the healing process. A therapist will feel something either negative or positive, and it is the same reaction for the client. So, it is important to figure out how to manage these emotions as early as one can, so that the intervention can be effective.

Counter transference is about how the therapist feels or reacts to the client. It depends on the, "ability of the therapist to discriminate accurately between feelings toward a client that are activated by client projections, and feelings better understood as having their origins elsewhere."[xii] The difficulty is to assess whether one is overwhelmed and whether one can process these emotions without being detrimental to the therapeutic relationship. I have had many situations at work that I am interested in probing or exploring further; however, I had to take a step back and reevaluate my position as a mental health professional by frequently asking myself these questions during the initial assessment with clients:

- Am I being effective or helpful to the client?

- Are these reactions a hindrance to the work that I am doing?

- Do I know when I am not being effective or when I am functionally impaired?

- Is the information I have from the client adequate to develop an intervention?

- Are my questions too many or could they cause harm to the client, and, considering what is being asked, what would be the version of the experience stored in our long-term memory?

What is noticeable is that through time and with greater experience, it is easier to judge. One will learn at some point how each encounter affects oneself with every new client. Eighteen months post-MSW degree, I was pretty sure what direction I wanted to go in terms of my career. I had applied to a PPSC program, was preparing for the CBEST, and was actively involved in the academic community (being a guest editor of an internationally well-known peer-reviewed journal, advisory board member, giving presentations, and submitting editorial comments, etc.). This route would lead me to an academic position while I was still working as a mental health clinician at the same time.

What stood out for me in my two-year experience of working with different population groups is how trauma impacted clients' daily lives. I was fortunate to work in at least six nonprofit agencies in two years and gained experience with foster care, residential services, school social work, veteran/military personnel, and homeless populations. Trauma work dominated all aspects of my work from clinical work to research and write-up. I had experienced trauma all my life, first growing up in a war-torn country and finally resettling in a poor urban community in the United States. I considered myself to be functional, but at times I am triggered by certain things that either happened in a session or by something somebody said, something unspecific, some words, or an association to an event. I never knew what triggered my negative reactions, which sometimes happened multiple times per day. Having a consistent and positive self-care practice is like building positive files in my brain I can access whenever I am triggered. Since being triggered is so unpredictable, I thought, and still do, that it is important to have good memories of each experience in conjunction with having a consistent self-care practice. I like to access past positive memories and experiences whenever I am triggered or under stress. This is what being functional and productive takes—the ability to maintain a sense of functional self despite struggling with clinical symptoms of trauma.

Self-Care Practice for Professionals

I discovered that it is easier to deal with clients and family members than professionals in affiliated fields. If you are working for a school, there are certain professionals that will drive you insane; either they are generally rude or they are incompetent and rude in combination. So, make sure you keep those who are professional and competent on your radar because they can be rare in any working environment. I learned to maintain this balance between insanity and sanity by keeping my emotional stability. Consistent self-care practice became a guiding light in my life when I first entered the field and continues to be important even after returning to academia.

One important lesson learned on burnout and managing negative stories from clients is knowing oneself. I learned this the hard way. It was with one of my last jobs when I hit my two-year mark of study for this project. Daily, I wanted to run away from the last job as soon I got there. It was not because I did not enjoy working, but it was this feeling of wanting to be somewhere else. This is an alarm for me. If I feel that I need to run to another place, it is a sign that I am reaching my psychological, emotional, and physical limit or threshold. I must find my way out or I will suffer emotional breakdown at some point. In recent years, this alarm is not feeling like I want to run away but rather feeling the need to sleep and relax. I also wonder if age plays a role in signals of exhaustion and burnout or if knowing that I have reached a level of professional pursuit I am satisfied with, makes these alarms different than before. Self-care helps in minimizing these negative feelings.

Self-care refers to the practice of caring for oneself to keep one's mind and body healthy. According to the University of Buffalo's social work department, self-care refers to activities and practices that one needs to practice on a regular basis to reduce stress and to maintain and/or enhance both short- and long-term health and well-being.[xiii] What does one do first? It is important to make a list of activities or things that (when reflected to past experiences) make one smile or bring back that warm giddiness of love and excitement. I often think back to what has worked for me when I was under stress. Some exercises that I find useful are discussed next.

Self-Care Practice 1: Walking and Talking to Oneself

The fact of the matter is that it takes great effort to focus on self-care with this type of work. Trauma requires a deliberate act of self-care, meaning that one needs to consistently take time for oneself. Me-time allocation should be a general standard of self-care practice. As a social worker and mental health clinician, it is important to feel healthy since the buck stops with the professional and not the client. In other words, one needs to feel sane, especially knowing that such a line of work will no doubt be directly involved in consuming vicarious trauma from clients. Physical and outdoor activities can help reduce some of these symptoms. Another problem in this line of work is that it requires me-time or self-care practice to maintain sanity. It is true that some people who go into this field—not all but a good portion—have experienced social injustice or trauma themselves and perhaps even were patients or clients themselves and have psychological vulnerabilities. A small portion of individuals perhaps are driven by their past experiences to have to understand what happens to a community or group that is inflicted by violence and has endured trauma repeatedly, and through time chose to get into this field. This is the reason that I returned to school to get a second master's degree, a degree that helps me understand who I am and how I can function as a survivor of atrocity and war. I wanted to do more than just trauma research. I wanted to get into interventions and preventions.

Self-Care 2: The Art of Smelling

The art of smelling takes on a different form for me for the two years that I was working in the social work field. I often notice blooms since I have enjoyed gardening all my life, especially adult life. After I became a mother, though, and while working in the field as a mental health professional, these blooms were more than smelling for pleasure and for simply dismissing quickly. I took great effort in seeking fragrant flowers, white ones mostly, to ensure that part of my self-care is aromatherapy. What does it mean to smell something that one can react positively to? It means a great deal in this case. It helps one to relax the body and mind momentarily. I deliberately plant fragrant flowers in various spaces in the garden, both front and back yards, for the purpose of having spaces to go to whenever it is needed.

A lot of social work is about learning to understand human complexity. As an anthropologist, I did know a few things about tragedies, living, and hardships, but some of these skills did not have appropriate names until I got training in the social work field. They all now have names, and because they have names, I know that self-care comes automatically. The year I started my second internship was the year that I started deliberately working on having a consistent self-care practice. Since I like gardening, it was natural that smelling was built into my self-care practice. I have always enjoyed gardening because it takes my mind off all life challenges. Once I became a social worker, I knew that I would need to deal with more than my own life challenges. In fact, I convinced myself that I did not have much time dealing with my own life until I embarked on my social work training journey. Like any hard swings of a pendulum, I went to one side and then moved to the other far end. In other words, I focused on others because it helped not to focus on me. The focus then was on trying to improve others' lives, not my own. I wanted to help others feel good about themselves. This task proved to be almost impossible at times because my daily encounters with clients seemed to affect my physiological well-being more than just the psychological and emotional. I was feeling sick, coming down with headaches, stomachaches, body aches, fever, cold, and cough. I spent as much time getting sick as I did feeling healthy. What saved me from falling off the emotional deep end was the garden, those spaces that I put in plants with fragrances. I discovered visiting these spaces regularly helps me to process, reflect, and regroup. I also feel rejuvenated after a short five or ten minutes sitting to soak in the fragrances and watching birds, especially hummingbirds, which frequent some of the blooms.

But this time, I had my smelling routine. I spent more time in the garden and started buying plants with sweet scents. A few seconds of smelling and touching were as therapeutic as doing a mindfulness exercise. I touched, rubbed the leaves and flowers, and took deep breaths among these plants at least twice daily, in the morning and late afternoon. Those seconds of soaking up sweet scents took me away and rejuvenated me whenever I had a rough day. I had many more rough days than not during the MSW Program, as well as the two years after.

Aromatherapy is an important part of my own self-care practice. I try to smell, feel, and taste things that are edible in my own garden. I also learned to recognize herbs and flowers that are edible. This way I can add to the list of things in my daily practice of self-care. Having said this, I also think that it is important to know yourself as you are; to know your limits, and to know what type of person you are. Some of us like to study people and prefer to observe, whereas others prefer to engage in activities or conversations with people. I tend to do a little of both. But my best decompression strategy comes when I am alone to think, contemplate, and explore nature alone. Some herbs and flowers that are easy on the nose and eyes include lavender, rosemary, honeysuckles, chives, oregano, basil, jasmines (lots of them), citrus blossoms, scented roses, and freesia. If you like to taste herbs and eat flowers, make sure you are knowledgeable about them, so you do not end up being poisoned by eating them.

One of the senses that people often ignore is sight. What you see plays a critical role in moods. Bright flowers make me smile every time. This suggestion may not work for everyone. Find your own shades of color. Find out what makes you smile. What I was told while growing up in this country is that colors have meanings. I do not know if people have reactions based on colors. I seem to have emotional reactions to some, but not to all colors. Purple flowers put me at ease. Yellow and blue flowers are happy colors and tend to be great for creating a positive mood. Grow nasturtium and squash. You can eat both. Putting colors in your salad will brighten your dishes. Do little things to surprise yourself because this is a good way for your body and brain to release a happy chemical (dopamine). I am referring to a neurotransmitter that plays a major role in reward-motivated behaviors (I will discuss this more in detail later in the chapter). In self-care practice, it is always important to learn about the science behind what is going on in your brain and body to use the information to your own advantage.

Self-Care 3: Recreational Therapy and Seeking Inner Self for Resources

According to the National Council for Therapeutic Recreation Certification, therapeutic recreation, or recreation therapy (RT), is defined as "a systematic process that utilizes recreation and other activity-based interventions to address the assessed needs of individuals with illnesses and/or disabling conditions, as a means to psychological and physical health, recovery and well-being."[xiv] Prior to entering the social work profession, I did not know how important it is to embrace the notion that consistent self-care practice is fundamental to this type of work. Unlike any professional discipline, it appeared to me that through the course of my training, including taking classes in traditional pedagogical settings, that a good portion of those trainers like me had prior experiences that forced or led them to the field (social work or other mental health fields). While this is not a bad thing, it takes a different mindset in terms of a professional approach to work or interact with colleagues. So, RT is useful for one's self-care and for the self-care of those one serves. The purpose of RT as a process is to "improve or maintain physical, cognitive, social, emotional and spiritual functioning in order to facilitate full participation in life."[xiv] It is about creating work-life balance to avoid burnout or emotional breakdown. This is real. In Europe, burnout is a formal diagnosis. We in the United States should certainly give this a serious diagnostic consideration since the working force generally is overworked and that people live to work, not the other way around.

There are a variety of techniques that a therapist could utilize to help reduce some symptoms relating to burnout. These include arts and crafts, animals, sports, games, dance and movement, drama, music, and community outings. I did not notice how often I integrated RT into my day-to-day activities until I learned it in the MSW program. The difference now is that I am doing it intentionally. I add RT to everything that I do after work. The gist of RT is to focus on what one enjoys doing the most and gives pleasure or joy. Or a simpler question to ask would be, "What gives me pleasure while doing it?" Consistency is critical because we all need to decompress at the end of the day, so we can be present and positive when we spend time with our children, spouses, and loved ones. At least this commitment to deliberately focus on making sure that I was healthy to be with people helps balance my mental health, feeling burnt out, and overall well-being. I do not view recreational therapy differently than any other therapeutic intervention, but I prefer to think of it as less methodological and more philosophical and emotional. In other words, I do what feels right. So, RT has become more an experiment, rather a scientific coping strategy, at least for me. I do not claim to be an expert on this approach in psychotherapy. I know RT helps improve symptoms of those living with schizophrenia and anxiety spectrum with severe symptoms (i.e., hallucination, intense nightmares, flashbacks, etc.). When I think of self-care personally, I often reflect on one specific hormone and a neurotransmitter. Both are responsible for the health and well-being of our mind and body. With this type of work, it is important to tap into our internal resources to make things work for us. We do not need external chemicals to feel good since we can get them from our own bodies (if we only know how). This is where self-care is more than doing things when we have time or can take a break. Its focus should be to make it intentional. This means putting work into it. In other words, we must do it intentionally on a regular basis.

Cortisol and Dopamine: Inner Self Resources

Two hormones are worth discussing here. One is cortisol. The other is dopamine. Cortisol can be called "enemy number one" for its destruction to our body. Both hormones are essentially like evil twins and play a critical role in making us happy, as well as creating problems for us in terms of causing diseases and mental health challenges from stress. The role of cortisol is not limited to helping our body respond to stress. Cortisol can cause diseases with too much stress.[xv] Understanding how these two chemicals work in our bodies can help us better understand the bigger picture of ourselves and how we can better address our own needs and therefore live a healthier life.

Cortisol is a primary stress hormone. Cortisol restrains functions that would be nonessential or detrimental to our immune systems. It generally enhances our brains' use of glucose and increases the availability of substances that repair our body tissues. It is a stress response, our body's alert system in a way. It is released from the adrenal glands in response to fear or stress as part of the fight-or-flight mechanism.[xvi] But when these stressors are present, and if we fear that we are under constant attack, this flight-fight reaction stays turned on. There is a long-term consequence to the brain. Long-term activation of the stress response system or overexposure to cortisol and stress hormones can disrupt all kinds of body processes. We can be at risk, for example, for having all kinds of health problems: anxiety, depression, digestive problems, headaches, heart disease, sleep problems, weight gain, and memory/ concentration impairment.[xv]

Dopamine functions as a neurotransmitter. It has a variety of functions but generally is the key in behavior, cognition, motivation, and rewards. Dopamine is released in our bodies. Imagine staring at a piece of chocolate and salivating over it. The brain releases dopamine as a response—those feel-good sensations that come from our brain to other parts of our bodies. It is a chemical in the brain that affects the emotions, movements, and sensations. It is not limited to these functions, however. It also associates with memory and pain as well as between certain negative actions and pleasure.[xvii]

I am talking about the idea of using or accessing what is available in our bodies, our own natural high, when I think of dopamine. We can access dopamine on a regular basis with the right consumption of food and other things (e.g., watching feel-good movies, listening to good music, and soaking sweet blooms). The question is how to access this hormone that is beneficial to us. One of the ways to access dopamine is through the selection of food that we know to give us pleasure. I selectively eat food that gives that extra boost of dopamine. I call it my own natural high. Tastes play a role in how we feel, as do all our senses. We react to things with our eyes. We also eat with our eyes just as much as our mouth. We taste food with our eyes. I go for both types of information when it comes to eating right to boost energy and motivation through the activation of my own feel-good chemical. There are a few food types that contain the right amino acids or antioxidants to stimulate dopamine production in our brains, which I will discuss next.

Reducing stress by whatever safe means seems to be key in our line of work. This is what I began practicing during the time I was trying to find myself by working for various nonprofit agencies (I lasted less than three months in some agencies). I balanced minimizing stress with increasing the level of the feel-good chemical in my body through eating food sources containing antioxidants and high in amino acids (like tyrosine) such as eggs, fish, chickens, and red meat. Some other food items include almonds, avocados, bananas, berries, and leafy greens. Watermelon, yogurt, milk, and green tea are supposed to contain important compounds as well. I fed my brain with greens and nuts, but my body with banana, berries, avocados, and fatty fish such as salmon.

As with anything we do in life, keeping a good balance means focusing on moderation. This has been a key to my success. I practice self-care that incorporates all kinds of things into my daily schedule, including exercise, gardening, listening to music, deliberately making myself discover new things in my own garden, in a grocery store when I go shopping, and taking time to dream and contemplate. I make all these activities a regular part of my day.

Self-care goes beyond daily exercise and being in nature; it should include food that the body uses to produce dopamine. A good life and work balance is about being intentional. If time is what is needed to ensure this balance, make time for these activities because they all matter in the long run. If one believes that there is not enough time in a day, one needs to take back that control, the control of one's time outside of the obligation such as work.

Conclusion

I highlighted some of the issues facing social workers and mental health clinicians, especially in our ability to practice self-care effectively. I discussed, for example, transference and counter transference and how we must be mindful of how we feel in our bodies and minds, and the need to take care of them on an ongoing basis. This chapter discussed self-care practice and the varied types of good self-care practice, as well as the science behind eating right and living a balanced life. Furthermore, I concluded this chapter with identifying food items that help our bodies activate our inner feel-good self.

The next chapter will focus on personal experience in a social work program and beyond. I will discuss what it means to change a career and the road to get to the destination or achieving that career goal.

CHAPTER 5

Career Change, Nonprofit Experiences, and Other Important Issues about Training

The hardest part of starting something new is how much patience it would take to get through daily. Patience was my best friend when I started this journey. It was something new, and I had no idea how things would turn out then. Unlike when I was younger, which came with idealistic impressions about life and career. Starting something new once I was already established in one field was extremely difficult. I was used to being independent and think like a professional in my own initial field of study (academic discipline). I had little success in using what I learned in social work because they (my superiors) did not recognize me as an equal nor did they consider I could contribute something significant to the new field. This was extremely difficult for someone like me who wanted to help and make myself useful. One important lesson to learn from such experience is patience. It takes time to build reputation and networks where I'd be seen for my skills and knowledge.

In this chapter, I will discuss trials and tribulations of working in a new career, provide pros and cons of working for a nonprofit agency and its general organizational structure/operations, and my own professional journey back to where I started twenty years earlier. I will start with a discussion on having a second career and the impact of a prior career on the relationships with supervisors.

PhD Degree is a Hindrance

The most difficult part about starting a second career was the treatment I received from professionals and inexperienced colleagues and classmates as coworkers (or worse yet, bosses). I had to eat a lot of humble pies, and I barely survived. I thought that I was prepared by being me because I know my own personality and know how to adapt when I need to. These skills (the ability to be flexible and understand changing circumstances) helped to a certain degree, but they did not always work when I was confronted with a treatment that I knew more about and the person supervising me knew a lot less. This was my reality for four years while switching between two social work programs, which made it difficult to adapt and adjust when things got tough. In hindsight, I should have conducted research studies on the emotional side of starting something new. Researching first about the new field of training, including mental preparation, and approaching with mental calculus, would be key to lessening the blow of encountering challenges. A good attitude was about eating a lot of humble pies. I did not have that good attitude. I thought hard work was all I needed to get through the training. Some of these experiences are highlighted in this chapter. These experiences serve as a focal point to the world of starting something new and of starting a new career in human services.

Too Much Knowledge is a Bad Thing

Starting over in the later years of life is generally difficult, especially when it requires going back to school. For me, it started with the first internship, and it went downhill from there, an experience that is difficult to digest even today. I had one clinical supervisor who preached (yelled) and demanded absolute agreement without questioning. I listened to the person in complete silence for fifteen minutes every weekly meeting. I learned fast by developing exit strategies even then. By now, four years post-MSW degree conferment, I have become great at developing exit strategies but for different reasons. At the same time, I began to realize that I was okay with change. What was disappointing was knowing such individuals thrived in this line of work and got to be in leadership positions. I came across a few professionals who were at this level of unprofessionalism. The professionals who were supposed to empower individuals, including youth, were oppressing the people they tried to train or help. This was mindboggling to me as a research social scientist and then as a social worker/mental health clinician. I could not understand how or why such a personality managed to find work in a field where compassion and empathy seemed to go a long way. In other words, it is easy to recognize that some of us will try to focus on failure instead of strengths of others. When we see the glass half-empty, we will run into more challenges. Every time I received a B grade, which I received for one class in the MSW program and one class for the PhD degree, changed the way I felt about successes, especially academic successes. My low self-esteem that I had thrown out the window returned with a vengeance when this happened.

The main reason I struggled initially in this new field was that I have been around (the block, the world, on the path or whatever the metaphor is) a few times. Career wise, that is. I thought that people would be able to take me and all my degrees and view me as an equal person. But I think people generally tend to think with a view of social comparison theory. Social comparison theory posits that "individuals compare themselves to others when they need an external standard against which to judge their abilities or opinions."[xviii] In other words, one will feel better about oneself if one feels less threatened and behave in a way that makes others feel oppressed. Compounded by power and control (if this person is your supervisor), what made it more challenging was the further negative reinforcement of group pressure that is created by this type of management style (autocratic and authoritarian) and the environment that was created by this type of leadership. Forcing others to conform to the supervisor's control is classic insecurity on the part of the person who micromanages the work. I felt then and believe now that displaying such forceful behavior to imply competence is problematic. One needs to know what purpose it serves first to engage in this type of behavior more effectively, perhaps in crisis situations where other lives are in danger and the aggressor needs to be controlled. What was left then was about feeding the "beast," figuratively speaking. Knowing what your potential supervisor needs and when to avoid conflicts is fundamental to your own success. I tend to choose the "give in now and save energy to fight another day" approach because it helps in the long run to avoid burning bridges unnecessarily.

Displaying a superficial "face" or imposter syndrome is an art form, which are skills I do not possess. I cannot act in this way. I need to be me, whatever that me is. It has always been my mantra that it is more important to be me and to be open and honest by being who I am than to display something that is not me. I remember what a coworker whom I worked with once said to me in a confidential tone. I could not understand why he was so bubbly all the time, smiling and greeting with the utmost manners and respect. He was always positive even when things were horrible. Five years later, after I left the organization and he too resigned and worked elsewhere, I learned his true feelings. I thought I went overboard with my assessment of the experiences at that agency. My description was not so colorful compared to the way he had perfected his French after he resigned from the agency. The gist of his feelings was that he felt smaller than a Thai phorid ant. A Thai phorid ant is just about 0.4 millimeters in length.[xix] It is the world's tiniest flying critter, which can sit comfortably on the eye of a common housefly. He said he hated every second of it (not the actual work but the people, specifically his incompetent boss) when he was at the agency. He said he could not be himself. He felt he had to put up a front to survive the workplace and gain the necessary professional experience to be competitive for future jobs. He said he was counting the minutes daily, until he felt that he had adequate professional experience, so that he could be competitive in the workforce. I concluded that this was what it took when one had no other options to support oneself. I was in his shoes when I was a lot younger, in my 20s and 30s, and certainly it was not a good feeling.

Inaction oppression came in many forms even in the most compassionate and well-meaning workplace. This type of oppression is often gotten ignored by employers because it is detrimental to them and their work. Young refers to this type of oppression as the "silent oppression."[xx] Silent oppression is about creating a culture that forbids employees to voice an opinion. People feel so oppressed and so powerless that they cannot talk at all. People have no voice and no will because of fear of losing their jobs. So, they cannot even address blatant injustices that are committed in the workplace. I have not had such an experience in a workplace since I usually develop exit strategies and run quickly before things get out of hand or I experience any blatant injustices.

Starting a new career is generally hard but more so when one has spent years in another field. Knowing how much one is willing to take is an important part of overcoming these challenges. This is important. Two things seemed to emerge during my journey, including the post four-year MSW degree: the mistreatment/negative experiences during the training of being an intern, and the "what in the world was I thinking" thoughts.

I started with a mindset that I was going to accomplish my goal and start my second career no matter how difficult it was going to be. It worked during the first round of training, starting with the BA degree, then the master's degree, and finally the PhD degree. This followed by being hired as a social science research scientist. But my ambition was different the second time around. This time it was not the jobs that I wanted to learn to conquer but the process. I no longer wanted to survive or sustain myself through forcing myself to stay at a job that gives me stress in order to pay bills. I did not want the stress or headaches of staying put just to ensure that I had a roof over my head and food on the table. I wanted to build a career as a social worker or mental health clinician, and at the same time I wanted to learn about the process. With my goals and objectives clearly set out before me, I was ready to embark on that journey. I also threw my negative self-esteem in a trash bin as I marched forward. One thing that seems relevant in life and in pursuing a career goal is to have clarity before starting that journey. I have accomplished this task by creating options for myself.

Experiences in Nonprofit Agencies: Board Structure, Funding Streams, and Other Issues

After I had gone through a good number of nonprofit agencies, I cannot deny the fact that I knew I was asking for some of these unpleasant experiences. I had embarked on a journey to understand nonprofit agencies, in part to understand the different levels of operations. Some have very strict funding streams and others' funding is generated from leases and rentals, fundraising via donations, or other means that required little oversight. By the end of the eighteen-month post-MSW, my decisions were sealed, and there was only one way in, one way out and away into an old goal. But first, it is important to note the importance of working for a nonprofit agency. It is not for everyone. It takes great strength and insight to determine what you need to thrive, and in my case, survive the ordeal as I embarked on untested, new, and unknown territory. I categorized nonprofit agencies into three areas: 1) small and new; 2) medium and established; and 3) big and complex.

Board Memberships

Regardless of the size of the organization, a nonprofit agency seems to select board members based on a transparent or purposive process that involved the best interest of its cause either through known affiliations recommended by other board members, or professionals known politically in a community that seems to have well-established relationships with other entities. An executive who works for a bank or a local politician is an example of this if a nonprofit agency is providing housing or housing-related services. This type of executive is generally a board member. Occasionally, a board would try something new such as selecting someone who does not have the capacity to do the work in the field. I had an experience in this in one agency. It proved catastrophic. The agency lost government funding and new funding opportunities were terminated prior to allocations even after it was awarded. Structurally, a nonprofit agency's board makeup is like a corporation except the board is usually in charge of appropriations and fundraising. The board drives the agency and the executive director reports to the board. The difference is in the financial compensations and ownership in the organization. The board in a nonprofit agency tends to have opposite responsibilities to a corporation board. Board members are not the majority owners in a corporation. Instead, the only stake these board members have is in their beliefs and passion in the work. They are committed to certain causes and view them as their primary responsibilities to ensure the agency's sustainability.

Fundraising is the single most important part of the board's responsibilities. In one nonprofit agency that I knew, a board member was required to donate quite a bit from their own personal accounts in addition to raising certain amounts from others. There is even a quota for board members in some agencies. They must raise certain amounts each year to be reselected or reelected. One of the more precarious positions of a board member is their relationship to the agency. Some board members became employees of the agency once their terms were up. I never knew what to make of this, whether through a lens of optimism or pessimism. If the glass is half full, then these individuals would be perceived as good since they knew what it would take to help reinforce or continue to promote causes and increase human capital for the agency. Since they were once board members, they are committed to the long-term sustainability of an agency. However, if viewed as a glass half empty, I can conclude that there is a degree of blatantly demonstrated issues of cronyism, nepotism, and corruption. There is a generally acceptable practice (lobbying) in any community for the purpose of benefitting the people who reside in the immediate area whether it involves environmental issues such as water rights in a rural community, or access to resources through redistribution such as school vouchers for those who live in a bad school district. In the United States, lobbying is a classic example of corruption. I had one interesting experience in a nonprofit agency, whose operations were difficult to comprehend, but this was their standard of practice. They tended to promote internally, and they tended to hire ex-board members as consultants, paying them handsomely (six figures for part-time work). In this arrangement, they treat newcomers as outsiders and in turn struggle with keeping frontline staff. It is like revolving doors. Their top positions remained with only people they'd known for a very long time, including ex-board members that became staff. In a bigger nonprofit agency, they tend to have built connections tightly with politicians. So, if one is new to the city, the chances of creating funding streams is quite small unless one has already established strong relationships with influential individuals, such as politicians if one is seeking government funding.

How does it work? There are both the short-term and long-term investment routes. The short-term version is about scaling up social and political influence. Imagine bodybuilders overdosed on steroids. That is probably what it takes to be competitive. Got the image in your mind, yet? One needs to work hard to get visible and make financial contributions to political candidates, and in the process, one hopes that there is visibility in the community of their work. How is this done? One needs to donate money to political candidates who may have power of the purse (at the local level this would be the county board of supervisors) and try to get them elected. If they are elected, then it is time to cash in through their sole responsibility as board members to make appropriations of government funding. I am familiar with the county supervisory board members because I had the opportunity to sit in meetings and discuss budget control and funding appropriations because of my role in a nonprofit that I worked for then. If they are elected, that county supervisor can designate funding through their annual budget for their specific causes or promises made during the campaign. A response for proposal (RFP) that is supposed to be open to the public or anyone who wants to bid for is not always open. Some agencies would already know the amount allocated to them prior to the submission of their grant application proposals. It runs deep in corruption and is quite subtle. It takes conspiracy for corruption in a developed world to happen. The meetings with these supervisors are closed door to let them know the amount they are receiving and, in some cases, not receiving for the year.

The long-term goal is to have homegrown politicians, meaning that they (nonprofit agencies) started recruiting youth from high school and trained them to become local political leaders by providing them with jobs and creating programs to keep them engaged, so they would return to the agency. This is a long-term investment. If one is investing this way, one is almost guaranteed loyalty. An agency that I got to know and involved with briefly committed to this goal. They were paid off when one of their homegrown youth made it all the way to becoming a board supervisor of a big city. One could only guess the cushiness that comes out of this investment. But again, who knows? I did not have an intimate enough relationship to learn the details of this type of investment, but there is for sure the "I scratch your back and you scratch mine" approach in practice, but I think you get the gist.

Large nonprofit agencies such as Kaiser, Sutter Health, and the like have complex systems and have created corporate-like environments with compatible pay and solid quality (high-caliber top executives to run) human capital. Kaiser pay scale for social workers, for example, is similar to the federal government, which makes them competitive with larger systems in terms of recruitment of qualified professionals. The smaller nonprofit agencies tend to advocate for competitiveness, but in truth some fall short in terms of compensation (both financial and in benefits). I have not been with a larger nonprofit agency such as Kaiser; my closest experience being a lifelong Kaiser member and knowing after twenty years the improvement they made to provide services. I remember in my early days how horrible it was to go to Kaiser in California. Once I got to Hawaii and became a member again, the Hawaii Kaiser was different. They were nice, helpful, and thorough. I was met with similar services and supportiveness when I returned to California a decade later. I do not have a problem with Kaiser anymore, but truth be told, one needs to advocate for oneself. Knowing what one wants will help guide one through the system and determine whether one's experience is good or bad.

I have more experience with nonprofit agencies than any other place, including academic institutions and defense contractors. I concluded that working for a nonprofit agency can be a good place for those who are looking for a fast-hiring process and just need a job or an experience in order to do something greater later in life. Unlike a government system, a nonprofit agency can hire someone immediately (in two weeks' time) once the folks in it determine the right qualifications. This is the positive side of applying for a job and wanting to work for a nonprofit agency. In a span of four years, I have worked for seven nonprofit agencies ranging in size from one with five full-time staff to one with over one hundred staff, and from about a million dollars in operating budget to over two hundred million dollars. These seven nonprofit agencies operate similarly, and all had some challenges. One major theme that ran through these nonprofit agencies was their public relations. One of them stood out for me due to the overall culture of operations. The staff seemed to be almost in a trance-like mental state and were afraid of the ED and deferred all decisions to this individual. The office culture was based on some interesting mixture of empowerment, loyalty, and extreme friendliness with an undertone of the action-oriented view of "you do, or you die" mentality. I felt immediately after a few weeks that I needed to run and run fast without looking back. With one foot in and one out, I knew that I could run when things seemed unsettled. I did just that with this agency. There were unethical practices such as claiming hours for no client appointments, and I was overwhelmed by this and others. The agency was forced to shut down because the agency's board decided to dissolve the agency but kept the school for an additional year. The ED resigned after the board discovered ten shell accounts with funding stashed in them. Schools that funded the agency demanded their funding back. The experience with nonprofit agencies led me back to where I started. I knew that I was going to return to academia someday, but I did not know that I was going to return earlier. I wanted to stay, collecting the clinical hours, which would mean I would have to work in the social work field, not teaching, an additional year.

Although I returned to academia in the end, I would not change anything about this journey. I learned a great deal. I do not regret spending six years building up the necessary skills to have a new career. I have become a better academic because I worked as a social worker. Social work allowed me to have that clinical dimension that I could not get as an anthropologist. As a social worker, I was more of an insider who was impacting change by working with one person at a time. As an anthropologist, I am more of an outsider who investigates and tries to understand a complex world of a community. Changing a career is about having an attitude and desire to change and knowing the importance of a career shift. I believe both of my degrees (social work and anthropology) are complementary, and each new degree helps improve my knowledge and refine my skills.

Culture of Nonprofit Agencies

Because of my limited time in working for nonprofit agencies, I could only get a good sense of a few of them, and some stood out for me more than the others. Some nonprofit agencies embraced the concept of beyond emancipation, restorative justice, or coaching method (trauma-informed care practice) with daily check-ins with staff, and others went all out by creating an impersonal corporate-like environment. The bigger ones seem to have the latter value in their office culture. The trends seemed to be creating a corporate-like environment of open-office spaces to give an impression of productivity and professionalism by putting up clear compartments to show people working (i.e., promoting productivity through peer pressure). Some went for a military style, placing computers about one foot away from each other and using long tables as desk spaces. It almost gave the impression of a start-up company that captured the essence of a new and entrepreneurial spirit.

The key takeaway was to reduce privacy, so workers were forced to work non-stop or pretend to be busy to give the illusion that they were working. Cubicles were seen as relics of the past, considered decadence of a bygone era. I was impressed by this physical type of arrangement, but the practices remained similar. Some new smaller ones still operated like the one that I worked for in the 1990s, with a cowboy approach of doing whatever it takes within the legal limit to provide services. Other bigger ones exercised restraint by creating rules and practices that were heavily bureaucratic that mimicked local government agencies. County agencies come to mind.

I did not get into this culture of a nonprofit in the early part of my nonprofit experience but did toward the end of my journey testing out nonprofit agencies. I was ready to return to academia by then and had no illusions about the challenges I had. The longer I stayed in a nonprofit, the more I felt that it was just time to move back to where I started after I received my PhD degree. The eight to five work schedules just did not fit me. I was too old and set in my ways or too independent or stubborn to change. This agency's culture seemed more of a cult than a working place, or at least appeared to act like a cult, especially in the way managers ran meetings. There was something uneasy about the format of a meeting that forced staff to feel awkward by forcing participation. There were only a couple things that bothered me at the time. One was this outcome-driven approach rather than meeting to make decisions to take actions on something or to provide updates. The meetings were more than a discussion about these key points. They included get-to-know-you sessions, a session on being effective at work, how best to support a coworker, and acknowledgements. The acknowledgements session was meant to highlight appreciations for coworkers and supervisors at the closing. What seemed to transpire were generally awkward moments for the staff. I rarely participated in these sessions. I kept wondering when these meetings would be over. The meetings occurred weekly and tended to go on for hours. The check-in session was the most exhausting and annoying. So was the appreciations session. I was sure that other staff thought the same thing. I thought of these questions: What makes you think we will be honest? It is a silly exercise. How much do you really like and appreciate your coworkers, especially with the kind of work we do? I was dealing with problems and people all day long, and I did not want to add more stress to my work. That was having to engage in touchy-feely exercises with coworkers and supervisors on a weekly basis and then get critiqued for the responses. At the time, I could barely stand my own supervisors and coworkers. I was sure the feelings were mutual. As much as I did not want to be there, they too did not want to be there to have to engage in these conversations. This was the hardest agency to work for. Reflecting now, I remember the interviews and how peculiar they were to me. I did question their method, but I thought we all worked differently. The executive director did ask during the initial interview if I checked in with myself every morning. This was a warning sign in hindsight.

One agency had routine training on self-reflection. Before I came onboard, something had happened, and I was told that it was more of a therapy session than a reflection. One staff member complained about the term "reflection" as having a bad connotation. I got confused over this statement. I tried to ask staff but generally got incoherent answers. I later learned that there were interpersonal conflicts between the staff. Having said this, trust was never a part of the equation in a workplace. If one thinks one can trust coworkers and supervisors, one needs to visit la-la land more often and stay there if one wants to feel safe. I believe that when I am at work, I am just another worker (this is about maintaining a professional identity). My personal identity is separate, and I share my feelings with my family, friends, and colleagues who are not working with me.

Work is not a place to share true feelings, in my opinion. I am a pragmatist unless some kind of harm may arrive as a result of change (e.g., the new hire is known to have caused harm by engaging in microaggressions). Then, I will let management know my personal feelings. We all made mistakes in this area. I certainly made my share of mistakes by trusting someone and getting myself kicked in the behind several times over. I even had one experience that cost me my job because I trusted someone who wanted my job much more than I did at the time. I quickly turned to exit strategies and began taking actions aggressively to run away from the place. I always had ongoing negotiations with other workplaces and put myself in a position of looking for a job by submitting applications even if I am not interested in changing jobs. One should never stop looking. I believe that it is important to be in a job search mode because one can feel more liberated by knowing and having options.

This was important to my mental health when I first started working as a social worker. In many ways, this is still very important to me now.

There are other agencies that I worked at that acted more "normal." They did not have this format for staff meeting. There was a simple meeting agenda to discuss specific things, updating each other on anything new (agency policies, upcoming grants), or organizing fieldtrips, etc. I am most familiar with this structure. They did some check-ins, but they were simple and were generally superficial. No one wanted to tell the truth of how they felt about work itself or their coworkers. Even when it was this straightforward, no one (including me) wanted to attend staff meetings. At the time of writing this ethnography, I decided to make a school-based psychiatric social work job as my last position before I returned to academia to focus on teaching and research full-time. This came with a price. A direct service position required one to do certain things that an advanced career professional would find stressful and annoying. In this case, it was clocking in and out hours daily. The strict working 8 to 5 schedules became a stressor and daily hindrance for me. I was not technologically savvy, with my outdated phone where the buttons no longer worked. I was struggling. However, I knew if I could hang in there long enough to get the clinical hours, I would be better off in the end. This was a short objective, which was manageable. I did not stay despite the desire to gain clinical hours to be qualified for the LCSW exam. I had to make up hours during my first years in academia by working in a private practice firm.

Conclusion

A key takeaway for me about having established a career in one field is that starting a new one is very difficult. The second lesson learned is that it takes a lot of time, effort, and energy, but more importantly, patience to start a new career. Even when one is doing well, one will always be perceived as a junior to somebody else in the field. In my case, I am a recent graduate and have not acquired my license in social work yet. So, that feeling is always present. I suppose the notion that there is always someone greater out there adds to our own insecurities. I learned then that it was not about being the best in the field but being the best one could be and having the satisfaction of being in a new field. The experiences and the relationships that came with meeting new people are worth the difficult journey. I was humbled, and sometimes it was painful. I took the best of the experience and ignored some that were detrimental to my well-being.

Chapter 6 focuses on one Master of Social Work program and the trials and tribulations of being a graduate student. Teamwork, network, conflicts, and academic politics will be discussed, as all of these issues weaved into the experience of the program.

CHAPTER 6

MSW Program

I was excited to do something other than writing and making presentations. I was also excited to utilize my skills as a social research scientist to impact change in a community. As an anthropologist, I have lived and worked in a community, whether abroad or in the United States. I always feel like both, an insider and an outsider in both my own community and in communities that I was not familiar with. Both perspectives grounded me in different ways and provided me with a different set of tools, which I have used in my life. As a young PhD, I was extremely insecure about my role as an analyst and observer even in a community that I have lived in and studied. Now, as a seasoned and experienced researcher (editing other scholars' work), I still am in many ways a learner of others' lives, their trials, tribulations, challenges, and numerous life transitions. Fitting in a new community is challenging in many ways. This is true when entering the MSW program.

Like a good student, I started reviewing requirements. I was excited about the prospect of absorbing knowledge presented to me by somebody else. So, with a high level of excitement, I was eager to start the quarter and my first year. I was in two programs: first in the full-time program and later in the part-time program. Both came with rocky starts. By the second year in the part-time program, I became a little more level-headed and felt grounded. By the third year, I became more selective and more aggressive in terms of things that I was willing to put up with. It took me four years and many trials and tribulations to get the degree. But I would not change any of my experiences. The following highlights some rewards and challenges of being in a MSW program.

First year in the Full-Time Program

The class that stood out for me in my first-year program was a class on race, gender, and inequalities taught by an inspirational soon-to-be professor who was writing his doctorate degree dissertation at the time. The lecturer was so inspirational that he made me miss teaching and being a member of a faculty team. Since then, I have been trying to understand my new career and role and what it means for my future career goal. At this point, I am not young enough to contemplate too long without seeing more gray hair, and that life would pass me by. This sentiment did not stop me from trying to have it all, a research/teaching career and clinical work. I have been involved in various projects and tried to take advantage of any opportunity related to my field, and at the same time moving forward by working toward planning how to gain clinical hours as soon as I graduated.

I took Human Behavior and Social Environment, Race/Gender/Inequalities, and field instruction classes to name a few and followed with other general education in social work. Some of these courses were not so interesting but were important to learn, such as human development courses and psychology theories developed by dead white men (Erickson, Sigmund Freud, Jean Piaget, and Lev Vygotsky) with an ethnocentric view of humans and skewed by their own ethnos lens as privileged white males, even in their time periods.

The challenge was not that I did not have what it took to be a student, but that I was too independent and strong-minded. I was generally influenced by my training as an anthropologist on how and what to study. This caused complications as I struggled the first quarter in the MSW program. Besides having to be a student all over again, I was also confronted with something that I did not like even when I was in the PhD program fifteen years earlier: group projects. I do not like to engage in group work because some of these experiences still bother me many years later. I did learn one thing, though, about group projects: tolerance. I learned to be more patient with diverse personalities. I had a project that I decided to do solo because the instructor agreed to my justification of the importance of doing this project alone. It was an advanced macro social work practice class. I learned by exploring the community that I grew up in alone and spent time on the project the way I wanted without the hassle of group dynamics.

First Year in the Part-Time Program

At the time when I started the part-time program, I was the only student who did not have a job. Classes were held on Saturdays and alternated with a hybrid class every other Saturday. So, classes started at 9:00 a.m. and ended at 4:45 p.m., two Saturdays per month and ended at noon on the other Saturdays. It was a long commitment to almost all Saturdays for three years. It worked well for those who wanted to keep working full-time. I was a mom then, and both my spouse and I were devoted parents. Even though I did not have a job when I started the part-time program, I still felt overwhelmed more often than not because of the amount of work involved, including internships. I was a new mom, so I still had to learn how to balance life and work (school) and struggled with adjusting to these new roles.

Second Year in the Part-Time Program

Second year was good overall. Because I was transferring from the full-time program, I had to start one quarter later. This means that I did not get to know the rest of the cohort. I was forced to get to know some of the new classmates. My struggles were with building and sustaining the different relationships with classmates, instructors, and colleagues in the field. I was having second year fatigue, the idea of feeling impatient and getting over it (MSW program). Several key points deserve some attention and are discussed below.

The classes were more interesting during the second year as the focus of the training moved toward social work practice. I was in the middle of Advanced Micro Social Work and group work classes when I realized that I did not know much about the social work practice. It is broadly defined to include individuals, families, groups, and an intermix of maintaining health and well-being and improving lives. This was the gist of my understanding. I took the class Advanced Practice in Social Work, which included group work. Even then, I was still waiting for that general framework for my future social work practice. I wanted to feel good about being a social worker, but that did not happen when I was in the MSW program. Traditional pedagogy is traditional, learning in a classroom setting. Reading and discussion of cases were the norm. I did not feel connected to the case or problem, as if I were living in a virtual, make-believe environment. Looking back, though, I did acquire the knowledge but not in the same way as if I'd met a person. That sense of connectedness to the problem and people offered a different view on reality. Their problems became my problems. Their world became my world. I was completely immersed in their daily living, their trials and tribulations. This was wisdom that I needed then, but I could not get in a classroom. I did, however, get some from the field experience (the best experience is from paid work, not internships).

By the end of the quarter, I was just happy that I completed the internship program at a big institution and was ready to start relaxing or at least did try to take a deep breath. I got immediately entangled with another project that consumed the final year of my internship. I was involved in consultancy work that almost derailed my goal and ruined my reputation as a result of the problems that the agency was having. I did learn a few things though, mostly about what not to do in a nonprofit agency from leadership down to hiring staff. I tried to stop the bleeding, but by the time I was fully hired, I could not change any part of the structure, and it was too late. The damage was done, and things went out of control. I was burnt out and left as quickly as I could without looking back. Again, like always, I had my exit strategies in place. I was aggressive in moving forward with plans B, C, D, E, and F. I got almost hysterical about the bleak prospect of the world in this field and began to be suspicious that people would know where I worked prior to applying for a job in the field. I began to think that I had no options except in academia. But by this point, I also felt I had no options in academia either, especially in anthropology since the national association that I belonged to opposed having anthropologists working for the military. The association holds the view of do no harm in a community one studies. I still held this mantra by advocating that the military should not harm a community and being an insider would help fighting for this more effectively; however, I was only one voice. I was losing this battle. I never wrote about the experience being in a war zone and working for the military. It was better to let those experiences rest in silence instead of providing a lens of the community and that part of the world to the outside world, in case what came out would do more harm. I still hold this view. The end of the second year proved to be productive. I did learn a few things about social work practice and working for a nonprofit agency such as applying theories effectively by learning the nuances of their applications. I was still on a high note and was eager to march on toward the final year with more enthusiasm and optimism.

Final Year

The final year proved to be very productive. By this time, I was already on my way to learning more about social work practice. One key point that stood out then was how to influence faculty about field instruction classes. Since the program required students to take field instruction for the entire last two years in a three-year part-time program, we were bombarded with case presentations and check-ins (our trials and tribulations in field placements). We had case presentations every quarter. There were three quarters per year plus twenty or more students. I was tired of how many case presentations we had to do per quarter by the end of the first quarter of the final year. I advocated for a change in class content and time from three and half hours to one and half hours. We did not achieve this goal to reduce class time in our field instruction classes at the time, but the future students were able to reap this reward. Their field instruction class time was cut in half. Even this experience seemed unimportant at the time. In hindsight, it was one of the best experiences in terms of advocacy work in social work. In addition, we became experts in case presentation.

There was one thing that I wished the training program would have provided in the beginning. That is a professional development seminar focused on the applications of theories (psychotherapy approaches) and discussions on strategies when working with clients. It would have been helpful to know how to tackle specific client challenges. I did not get to learn theories in clinical treatments until the last quarter in the final year, for example. By this time, I had fully grasped what I thought I would need to be successful in getting employment after graduation in terms of knowledge about theories. The emphasis in the training leaned heavily on ethics and law. Also, epistemology of social work, specifically practices on professionalism, seemed to be the focus of the training since they were introduced in all classes in a subtle way. Why is this important? A seminar focused on being a professional social worker allows students to begin thinking about how they should frame the fundamentals in social work practice. It would be useful to have broad training across the field in a quick and dirty fashion during the first year where students would get some information on a lot of areas of social work practice to steer them to the right path.

I had Advanced Practice in Social Work during the last quarter. This was where the ah-ha moment took place for me. The instructor introduced various theoretical orientations. Some were interesting and others were proven to be useful. Unfortunately, the faculty who taught our class was new to teaching and at a master's level. She seemed generally confused about how to apply theories in a clinical setting. I learned more from reading the books and asked those who were working in the field.

CBT, IPT, DBT, You, and Me

The final year, or advanced year, was when the fun began. Prior to this year, the training appeared to be too disconnected from the field and practice. I did not know what my theoretical orientation should be nor could I articulate what I should use in counseling, and I didn't know the difference between psychotherapy and counseling. So, learning about CBT, IPT, and DBT, for example, came much later in the advanced year of the program, mostly through field placements (not from classes). I remember during one of the meetings that I attended for my internship, someone asked me about my theoretical orientation. I was not new to learning the pros and cons of using a conceptual framework for my own research studies. I stalled for time and said, "I am still exploring my favorite one." I had no clue then what I was talking about. I figured buying time and learning about it later would at least save my reputation temporarily. I was never asked to explore some of the theoretical orientations and learn the pros and cons and why they were relevant to develop treatment plans or important in interventions. Having said this, this was a social work training, not other counseling or psychotherapy-focused training. Social work is more general, and the degree is terminal. Social work focuses on helping individuals, families, groups, and communities to improve their individual and collective well-being. This definition was too broad for trying to find tools to use for interventions or solutions. Broadly speaking, the definition of social work is difficult to define precisely like the definition of anthropology. The National Association of Social Workers begs to differ with my statement. However, it is not easy to define what social work is, and it seems easier to talk in terms of social work practice. The core of the practice is guided by the core values of service to community, social justice, and the dignity or worth of every person.[xxi] The application to clinical social work is in the approaches used in psychotherapy that has its root in psychology, which will be discussed as follows.

Cognitive Behavioral Therapy (CBT) came much later in the advanced training. In my case, I had the class in my last quarter of the program. By this time, I'd completed all my internships. Beck Institute defines CBT as a "time-sensitive, structured, present-oriented psychotherapy directed toward solving current problems and teaching client skills to modify dysfunctional thinking and behavior." This came with key terms such as cognitive formulation, case conceptualization, cognitive model, and automatic thoughts. Beck Institute defines cognitive formulation as "the beliefs and behavioral strategies that characterize a specific disorder." The definition of case conceptualization is described as an understanding of a client's specific beliefs or patterns of behavior. Cognitive model is defined as "the way that individuals perceive a situation is more closely connected to their reaction than the situation itself." [21] The intervention is focused on building one's skills to live an independent and self-sufficient life through helping a person identify and change troubling emotions, thoughts, and behavior. This definition seems to encapsulate the various aspects of a person and their totality and the intertwinements of external influences (e.g., beliefs, values, and practices).

Another approach that is known to be effective for depression is IPT. I used IPT several times during the training, but I was never comfortable with it, partly because I was uncertain about the symptoms or the diagnosis at the time. Interpersonal Therapy (IPT) is defined as "an empirically validated treatment for a variety of psychiatric disorders."[xxii] It has been known to be used for a variety of disorders, such as anxiety disorder and eating disorder that is recognized as an efficacious psychotherapy by the American Psychiatric Association and the American Psychological Association. It is one of the few models that leans on a biopsychosocial, cultural, and spiritual model. Its underlying assumption is that interpersonal distress results in psychological symptoms. I have used this model several times on several clients. It seems to work best with depression. I have not tried it on eating disorder or anxiety spectrum.

Finally, I was lucky to receive training on Dialectical Behavior Therapy (DBT). DBT is a "comprehensive, evidence-based treatment for borderline personality."[xxiii] This theoretical orientation is known to be used for borderline personality or identity related problems. I discovered that DBT is quite difficult to use simply because of its various components:

1. Serving the five functions of treatment,

2. The biosocial theory, primarily focusing on emotions in treatment,

3. A consistent dialectical philosophy, and

4. Mindfulness and acceptance-oriented interventions.

I had one-day training but never had the opportunity to use with clients effectively until a few years into the clinical work. According to the National Institute of Mental Health, borderline personality disorder is defined as a "mental illness marked by an ongoing pattern of varying moods, self-image, and behavior."[xxiv] The main symptoms include impulsive actions and problems in relationship with intense mood swings between anger and depression or anxiety. Because of the nature of these symptoms, there is a higher degree of complexity and difficulty working with people with this diagnosis.

Furthermore, it takes energy and patience to deal with emotions. This is what I discovered when I started working as a clinician. I am usually drained with a few cases, especially those that involve lots of emotions. However, the most difficult part is not diagnosing, it is telling the clients that they need to try different strategies. Those clients who did well tended to try different intervention approaches. At the same time, clients who resist trying seemed to show a lack of progress in reducing symptoms. I used the analogy of old worn-out clothes that are kept in a closet and taking up space. I used this analogy to explain the reason for sharing their problems. It is the same as an "out of sight, out of mind" approach. I would explain that they needed to talk about their problems, so they could feel better because all our emotions need to go somewhere. In this case, they needed to go through our bodies like old clothes that we throw away. Therapy or counseling is about purging thoughts from our bodies. We must find ways to remove them from our brains. One of the ways is talking. Another is journaling. This is how I frame therapy because it is the truth.

Me and Therapy

Of all these theoretical approaches, I discovered that CBT is easiest and most useful to develop interventions and case formulations for. I stopped counting a while back when I asked a social worker or mental health clinician what theory they used in their practices, partly because the consistent answer was "huh." CBT became this acceptable and unquestionable model for treatment. CBT has various components including cognition, behavior, and emotions. So, I have learned that what I view to be most useful in terms of approaches in psychotherapy may not be anyone else's ideal theoretical model. It takes time to feel what is right and what works for the kind of clients being seen by a particular therapist. Reading about the subject can only take us so far, but practice helps inform what works best with what symptom.

Bottom line is that one needs to start early to find out what one's cup of tea is. In other words, it takes time to understand a theoretical orientation and how to practice effectively or claim it. I learned that to be effective is to do more than research. It takes practice, talking to mentors or those who are in the field for a long period of time. Human behaviors are complex and there is no one shoe that fits all. In my case, I got to learn about these different models and how they applied to psychotherapy from reading and talking to colleagues and mentors and through practice with clients.

Conclusion

In summary, social work training is not the same as other psychology-related fields such as Marriage and Family Therapy (MFT) or general counseling training. The MSW degree is a terminal degree, and skill-building in counseling and psychotherapy plays a small part in it. That was my experience in one MSW program. The point is that it is best to explore what one wants and what each program offers.

The next chapter focuses on different experiences with clinical supervisors. I had some good ones and some bad ones. The more experienced field instructors are more reflective and refine their approaches to teaching. The next chapter will highlight these keys points of field placements and internships and the roles of field instructors.

CHAPTER 7

Clinical Supervisors

At first glance, it did not seem important to have a personality match when it came to a clinical supervisor. Clinical supervision dictates one's experience as a clinician and a social worker. A positive experience from a clinical supervisor will set one off on a good start. On the other hand, a bad one can be damaging and make one cynical. This is about avoiding burnout midway through the internship or rupture in the relationship with a field instructor. Indifferent clinical supervision experience is when they care less about their role in the field education. In this chapter, I am detailing three types of clinical supervisors to give an understanding of the need to make the right choices.

Clinical Supervisors: The Good, the Bad, and the Indifferent Management Styles

One of the most challenging experiences is finding a fit with one's clinical supervisor. This means that both personalities must fit in a way where one's working style and the other person's working style are in sync. I am referring to both individuals sharing that unspoken level of comfort with interactions at the field site. Taking suggestions is generally uncomfortable, but there is a higher level of discomfort if there is a need to question the clinical supervisor's judgment by the intern. This is about management style. Some managers like to micromanage—the inability to let go and feeling the need to be in control of the work. This treatment is oppressive for individuals who like to have independence and need only minimal guidance. One can feel trapped at times if one feels someone else dictates every aspect of the job. So, knowing one's own personality and how one is functioning at a job will be half of the battle to safeguarding sanity.

Micromanagers involve different types of management styles. Some of them can be aggressive and seem to offer general nonconstructive suggestions. An example is criticism that leaves one paralyzed, and feeling small after every clinical supervision. If stuck in this type of situation, adjust your engagement style until it can be figured out how to minimize that experience. However, it is difficult to see what is happening in a situation that one is a part of and be objective at the same time. In many ways, interning is time-limited, so persevering until the end of the internship is an option. Another option is to take quick actions to look for another internship or another clinical supervisor. This latter option is usually difficult. In my case, I had one clinical supervisor who was aggressive and uncaring, mean, and direct in approach. For example, I went and conducted a home visit. The client was still sleeping, according to their mother. Without allowing me to explain what I did after saying this much, this person said, "You need to stay with the mother. Talk to her. Build rapport. Ask for a cup of coffee. Sit in her living room and talk to her." In our first few initial clinical supervision meetings, I would remain quiet instead of explaining the home visit. I kept thinking about how I did all of that, including inquiring about the client and asking if there was anything else that I could do to help her to get the client out of bed on time for the appointment. But instead of explaining, I kept silent and refused to engage with this clinical supervisor. Another example was providing my own assessment of my work performance. I told them that I did not know how to assess myself when I spent all my time working with clients, traveling between three schools, and dealing with crises. My point is that some clinical supervisors are extremely rigid and insensitive to the needs of the interns and staff. Some refused to acknowledge their own counter transference and used the clinical supervision time channeling their own negative energy. Mine was unfortunately extremely rigid, argumentative, rude, and insensitive. This person would not allow me the space and time to explain my own strategies but instead would choose to assume and criticize my actions. This kind of supervision was paralyzing at times. So, it is important to find that person who matches one's own style and personality to avoid secondary trauma. Social work is itself traumatic, emotionally draining, and demanding. Best practice is to know oneself enough to eliminate any possible personality clash.

There are other managers who enjoy macro-managing and use some gentle approaches to correct mistakes. These are the types that allow new and lesser experienced staff to flourish in a working environment (if the new staff are competent and have the necessary skills). There are problems with macro-managers too. The hands-off approach only works with some. Some need guidance and at times handholding to get through or build new skills. I am self-driven, so macro-managers are a good fit for me. In fact, while I was looking for an internship (after the first two bad experiences), I made decisions based on my experience dealing with field instructors. I asked how they managed interns and staff. I asked for an example when it worked well and when it did not work out and what happened to that person. This information helped inform my own decisions about whether I could work with a field instructor.

The third type of management style is the indifferent one. This is about depending on one's own skills and knowledge to get the job done. This type tends to have extreme professional boundaries. They would not interact with staff or interns at work unless it is in a meeting or when discussing cases. I had one clinical supervisor who stared at me during our weekly clinical supervision and barely asked any questions about my caseload and didn't offer any suggestions. Occasionally, the person would send me an email about a workshop or training that I should attend but offered no guidance in terms of how I should fund these activities. This same person would not eat or socially interact with me during internship hours. In fact, the person would try to avoid any interactions outside those few commitments (e.g., weekly clinical supervision, weekly team meetings, and weekly joint assessment meetings).

Depending on one's working style and sensitivity to suggestions, one of these three types can help one succeed and give that positive experience or fail. In an internship setting, the experience can cause an intern to change his or her mind about continuing with the MSW program. Personally, I discovered that the macro-management style with a gentle corrective approach works best with me. I am sensitive and independent. I do not deal well with a direct approach from a supervisor or those who try to control me. I had one supervisor who provided me an hour-by-hour daily work schedule, including times for a bathroom break and lunch.

Generally, it is difficult to do due diligence about one's working style and a potential supervisor's working style. There is not much an intern can do in the way of choosing the right field instructor. One hopes to get something that is worthwhile at the end. The only thing that is left is to garner first impressions during an interview. So, the assessment of fitness will be limited, which leaves one with relying on instinct and intuition for what one cannot know. It is different with real jobs. In most cases, I was able to know by the third month if I could stay or must leave, which was often at the end of the probationary period of most jobs. If I feel things are not going in my favor, I develop exit strategies and begin taking actions to provide myself with options. Plus, taking actions to change one's current position is therapeutic.

MSW Program Clinical Supervisor

Interning or working for free takes a different mental state. I really do not know anyone who spends 16 to 24 hours a week working for free, especially if they are living paycheck to paycheck. The first year of an internship normally is scheduled for two full days per week and the second or final year is typically three days a week, or 24 hours. Some field placements provide flexibility in how an intern can accrue hours per week with some kinds of arrangements with the field instructor, but others may not or are rigid on how they want to use their interns. Being an intern is difficult because staff's perceptions generally leaned toward the negative side instead of a positive one, including the importance of interns' contribution to their professional progress. Chances are that most staff would view having an intern as something they have to deal with because they were told so by their superiors unless the superiors are committed to supervise the interns. As an intern, I felt a sense of displacement, an outsider or someone who was there to be in the way. What I meant by commitment by superiors is that some agencies, whether it be local or federal government agencies, use interns as a form of recruitment for maintaining, expanding, or fulfilling current/future vacancies. In this case, supervisors do invest in interns. The next few sections will highlight some of these issues, especially the role of clinical supervisors in helping interns' growth in the field.

Eighteen Months after the MSW Program

I have had three clinical supervisors in the MSW program. The first two clinical supervisors were the ideal type that anyone would like to have as future mentors for the rest of a professional career. One that I had I would not wish upon anyone and kept wondering then, and still now, how in the world they ever got into the field to begin with. There was no compassion or gentleness. I heard horror stories about clinical supervisors and how they treated interns and new clinicians who were working toward clinical hours to qualify for the LCSW exams. I encountered one that was horrible. The person was stoic, negative, and rigid. It was the first time I felt my dream of being a clinician or therapist was in jeopardy. All these experiences taught me how to put clinical supervisors into specific categories as I will discuss next: the good, the bad, and the indifferent.

The Good Clinical Supervisors

I discovered that good clinical supervisors tend to exhibit compassion, are strict but with a gentle soul, and demonstrate a lot of empathy. I had several good clinical supervisors. One clinical supervisor I had was during the last year of the internship and two were from after I graduated with the MSW degree. The one that made an impression and changed the path of my social work career was the clinical supervisor in my advanced year internship. She was inspirational and supportive. She knew how to get the right people for the kind of support an intern needed. Her focus was to produce the kind of school-based social workers that would have long-lasting effect on a young person's life. This was her objective. I was pleased that I had a better year at last from someone who knew something about being a social worker in a way that helped a new social worker see what lay ahead and what to expect in the future of social work practice.

We had weekly individual supervision to discuss complicated cases. I will not go into detail since I discussed some complex cases elsewhere already, but it was the kind of environment that allowed me to feel safe and secure enough to discuss the challenges and successes with this person. Also, the person was never critical or judgmental about my failures or lack of success with students or of interventions or treatment plans. We did not diagnose any students since this clinical supervisor did not believe in labeling students with a disorder. Bottom line is the person made me feel safe about discussing clinical issues or challenges in our individual supervision. In our weekly group supervision, however, we discussed complex cases and attended seminars on various topics. One that stood out to me was on self-care and trauma training. Occasionally, we had training on other topics such as psychodrama, CBT, or writing self-care prescriptions. We also had field trips to various places. One was on play therapy with a therapist who practiced from the residence. I had never seen a library full of dolls and figurines before then. The place had many other toys and tools that I did not recognize but seemed interesting to play with. Some of them, such as sand trays and hour glasses, were placed in different rooms to create a playful environment. It almost felt like children's Fairyland but fit adults too. It was a rather cool way of displaying tools for therapy. It opened my eyes to the possibility of play therapy as part of my future interest in clinical social work.

Since that experience, I have had other opportunities that did not give me that good or solid feeling of what it means to feel as a social worker. Still, I was inspired because I felt like I could make a positive impact on clients, being in that supportive relationship with a clinical supervisor. I felt safe with this clinical supervisor and a few other supervisors whom I met and worked with during the post-MSW degree years. What made all the difference was my interest in working with children and students. While I continued to convince myself that the work was anything but, I did embark on experimenting with different areas of social work.

The Bad Clinical Supervisors

One of my clinical supervisors threatened to not sign off on my hours when she wanted something changed. Fundamentally, there is something wrong with this approach, and it shows a lack of compassion and dignity. The bad ones exhibited these qualities (microaggressions) but also had other problematic character traits, for example, outward ruthlessness, lack of compassion, a judgmental approach, and the tendency to assume. This type tends to have extreme demands. I discovered that leveraging what I had was critical when it came to this type of behavior. In this case, it was about clinical hours that I felt I had a lot to lose in this situation. I remained silent during the entire internship and put my head down to finish up the hours.

One of the more challenging experiences is having to deal with one's own feelings regarding what is important in one's career. I was new to this field and felt the brunt of what the military called second, third, and other orders of effect, which means facing various consequences or negative experiences as a result of the initial action. I had one unfortunate experience midway through collecting my clinical hours that was unpleasant. The person had unrealistic demands that would cause me to feel unsettled. It was the first time in my life where I felt oppressed and depressed at the same time, mostly anxious about the prospect of having to deal with this person. I had to develop an exit strategy at the time. I was too far along, getting the hours, to quit the job. Developing exit strategies is nothing new to me; however, the timing of it was new. This person demanded a caseload with detailed information of each student, which I found unacceptable, unrealistic, and unusual. This person demanded information that one could not obtain at the initial contact or assessment. In addition, the person demanded that I itemize hours in a day that I spent doing certain things, including whether it was traveling, face-to-face, assessment, research, collateral, or other services. What happened to our honor system? Prior to this experience, this person flat out threatened me about the hours if I were to be late for meeting with the person and this was after I was stuck in traffic due to an accident on my way back from one of the three schools that

I was responsible for. After this experience, the person lectured me about what I needed to do during a home visit but without asking what I had done while conducting a home visit. During the fourth session, this person scolded and lectured me for about twenty minutes on how I should 100% embrace their assessment without my own assessment on the clients in my caseload. Besides, this person never met any of my clients. As a researcher, I always believe that two opinions make a result stronger, but more opinions would be even better. Unfortunately, this was not the case. Also, this person accused me of not believing in the assessment because I had another agenda. In my mind and silence, I kept thinking that I was not going to allow this person to prejudge me or my clients. I struggled with this. But what was most disturbing in this relationship was that our personalities clashed. I tended to be a bit more compassionate and sensitive about what I say and do, especially with the clients in my caseload. I do not do well with negative reinforcement. This person operated under the assumption that proof matters more than the honor system and productivity was irrelevant. Their approach seemed to assume guilt, and force you to prove your innocence. In contrast to my point of view on this matter, I tend to trust what you tell me unless you prove me wrong. I remember feeling that there was no light at the end of the tunnel when I was still immersed in this. I felt trapped, oppressed, and in a way, emotionally abused. I felt bad the entire time, from that first weekly supervision meeting until the last. The threat of not signing my weekly hours became this roadblock that I could not see beyond. This person's control and power affected me and my work with clients. At the three-month review, this person used our discussion that I initiated and wanted to discuss the different treatment options as areas of improvement in my own performance review. This person confessed to never administering assessment tools (e.g., PTSD checklist, Beck Depression Scale, etc.). On top of this review, this person suggested an area of improvement to include countertransference. This suggestion caught me off guard, simply because I was the one to tell this person that I needed to do a bit of self-care since I was dealing with too much vicarious trauma during the week. I truly believe that everyone has that breaking point or red line that cannot be crossed. Mine happened when this person threatened to not sign off on my clinical hours. These suggestions, which were mine, added to the mix of the performance review of my job pushed me to the breaking point. The weekly supervision became an unsafe space for learning by the third month into the job. I knew I had to leave quickly. So, my exit strategies were implemented in earnest at this point. I never stopped looking for a job and was always in negotiations with other organizations. Of the three months of meetings with this person, I did not ever see a smile. By this time, I became even more aggressive in the process of finding a way out. While the relationship with this person seemed to become more intolerable each day, I did enjoy working with youth. Some youth have tremendous challenges, and one might wonder how they could still thrive after all their negative experiences. In this sense, I was able to focus on my work with them and made that part of my job a positive experience.

The Indifferent Clinical Supervisors

This type of clinical supervisor comes with two distinct personalities, but it essentially involves a major nonresponsive or hands-off approach to providing clinical guidance. If one were to encounter this type, one would pretty much be alone with the clients. One colleague of mine described her internship experience like this: "Here's the work and don't ask me any questions." She said that she didn't see her clinical supervisor until her last meeting. There was no weekly clinical supervision or guidance. She felt the consequences if she were to ask for guidance. As an intern in a program such as this, one does not generally encounter threats, but occasionally it does happen. It is bad. The other behavior in this category is "missing in action" (MIA). I think that the indifferent type of clinical supervisor, in many ways, is more detrimental to the health and well-being of a soon-to-be mental health clinician. But then again, it depends on one's own personality. If one needs help and tries to seek support from an indifferent person, one may not get very far. But if one is the type of person who wants to be left alone and independent, then they may not be bothered by the indifferent type. I had a colleague who tried to start her second career and was assigned to this type of clinical supervisor. She was in her advanced year and was struck by her new experience of how difficult it was to deal with this type of supervisor. She decided to do her advanced year with the same nonprofit agency but wanted to focus on a different population and area of social work. She was placed in another city and in a different unit, which focused on behavioral health and not end of life care. She had to find another placement midway through the quarter and make up the hours because she could not tolerate the indifferent and hands-off type of a clinical supervisor (her field instructor).

Some MSW programs are better at managing expectations and engaging with field instructors, but there are others that just do not do a good job at advocating for students. In other words, these latter programs tend to perceive the importance of maintaining good relationships with field agencies instead of supporting students. Some MSW programs are sticklers about their policies. The program that we were in, I could not bank my hours, but I could increase the number of days to get extra hours to make up for any lost time. I had to make several changes during the program. In my case, it was first the full-time program and then entering the part-time program. My experience was different than my colleagues in both programs. Either way, when something does not feel right, it is important to get out fast. This was my mantra. In many ways, it is still my mantra. I generally know about three months into a job or role if it is going to work out. With the previous job, it turned out to be the shortest tenure I had. I quit after three and a half months into the job. I did not feel right from the beginning, but I wanted to give it a chance, knowing little about the agency. I did not do any research since it was based at an old high school. My goal was to return to work at a place where I started learning English and felt that I was integrated into a mainstream American community.

Since I have also believed in developing exit strategies or always have a plan B in place, I am already in negotiations with other agencies even as soon as I start a job. More times than not, an offer would come right before my resignation. The above job that I used as an example was the first time where I did not give a two-week notice. The reason was that I did not feel that I was being treated professionally by upper management. This included their inability to provide support for me and my one staff member at the time. I left the same day I accepted another job offer. It felt good to be able to walk away with minimal emotional investment at the end. I did not feel guilty for leaving a job simply because I did not think that I caused damage to the people I served and to the program by my absence. I did not have time to build relationships at work given the short amount of time spent in the agency.

By the end of the second year, the focus shifted. I was done with learning to understand nonprofit agencies. I had only one objective at this point. I was looking for ways to return to academia. Having said this, I was about to embark on another journey with another nonprofit agency. But I was more realistic now with one specific goal. I was going to stay until I accrued enough clinical hours to take the exam. This was clear to me even if I were to return to academia. I was wasting my time, according to my own calculations. I should have gotten at least 50% of the total hours required at the end of the second year after I received my master's degree in social work, but I was not where I wanted to be (three years are generally needed to accrue the 3,000 hours for the LCSW exam; it required 3,200 prior to 2018). I'd quit a third job so far, and it was only about eighteen months after I graduated with the MSW degree (this was intentional because I wanted to learn about the different areas of social work such as child welfare, forensic, medical, etc.). While hours can be accrued during the coursework in other counseling-related fields such as Marriage and Family Therapy (MFT) or another psychology-related degree, this was not the case with the social work degree. I was too slow to learn the ropes. Some people view this approach as all or nothing. I could not lie to myself about being authentic or genuine about the work and people. At this point, it became clear to me what social work entailed and that the road to practice meant different things to different people with different experiences. By the end of the third year after I graduated, I accrued enough clinical hours to qualify for the LCSW exam and I was offered several academic positions. That fall (August 2018), I returned to academia. I was ready to put my research of working for nonprofit agencies behind and move back to the comfort (or craziness) of academia where I feel I belong. The last clinical supervisor was the best of them all. She understood her role as a clinical supervisor while most others were not good.

Conclusion

Unfortunately, it is difficult to assess what type of clinical supervisor is good or what type is not so effective in the end. There is not much in the way of choosing or making a decision as an intern since most decisions rest with the management. It is really a matter of chance. Knowing when to look for something else is more important because one can always make up the hours later. In addition, one can learn more about what not to do. The only disadvantage of having too many bad ones or indifferent ones is about having to make up the hours. As an ACSW or board registrant, it is about putting one's own clinical hours in jeopardy through delays of licensing. In short, it helps to have a good clinical supervisor who can coach how to effectively work with clients, the complexity of human behaviors, and their social environment.

In this chapter, I discussed good, bad, and indifferent clinical supervisors. I started by saying personality match was the most important attribute if one wants to survive the first several years as a new social work practitioner. I detailed my personal experiences of having multiple clinical supervisors from my experience as an intern to a professional social worker in the field. I concluded with the importance of knowing one's own path and goal to reduce deterrents or the chance of getting off track when pursuing that career dream.

Chapter 8 focuses on fitness, and that is job fitness and client fitness. It takes time to figure out who to work with and whether a client and social worker are a good fit. I offer personal experiences and specific examples for a deeper understanding in the next chapter.

CHAPTER 8

The Post MSW Degree Experiences

My exploration for a fit between a clinical supervisor and me did not stop after I graduated from the Master of Social Work program because the knowledge of accruing over three thousand hours to qualify for the social work exam was painful. I continued to struggle with a job that came with a clinical supervisor who did not understand my needs and how I functioned in the field of social work (not as a newcomer in the social work field but an experienced professional in another field). One of the ways that I have struggled with this throughout my life is this constant need to seek or focus on career choices. I do see that such career exploration should end at some point and that it should be a forever exploration of a journey. I tried to reframe that I was embarking on a mission to find out what social work was and what I could do to contribute to this field in a more meaningful and effective way. There is a reason why my journey began and ended in academia as a faculty but midway through was something else such as an advocate, interventionist, and a mentor. While I am experimenting in the field of social work through changing and applying for various jobs, I am keeping a record of these experiences to assess the long-term impact and what my contribution will look like in the social work field someday. This started with a frontline job, fresh off the master's degree program, where employers loved to take advantage of the inexperienced folks by paying minimally and getting so much more in the process. This is usually for about two years before a social worker gains adequate experience to get another job that pays a little better. As of 2021, Bank of America, for example, sets $25 per hour as its minimum wage. This was the hourly rate when I got my first job offer after I received my degree in social work.

First Social Work Job

At the time when I was writing my master's degree thesis on trauma affecting Asian Americans and Pacific Islanders in the San Francisco Bay Area, I was consulting for a mental health agency that was in upheaval, politically and contractually. I was also offered a job to do pretty much everything from managing staff to writing grant proposals, running and sustaining programs, to developing new programs, providing training to and recruiting staff. I took the job with the notion that there was no way that I could not fix an agency that was about to go through a free fall without a point of return. I tried to salvage what was left but failed in the end.

While I worked full-time doing everything to keep the boat from sinking, figuratively speaking, I had my exit strategies in place and took action to give me options in case I needed to resign at any moment (the county was threatening to end the contract). Since it was based on annual contractual renewal, the political climate of the agency would also ensure that it would fall on any given working day. I applied to two jobs; low level as a case manager for a foster care agency. I was interviewed and offered one of them. My salary was reduced by 50%, but it had a flexible work schedule. I was keeping an eye on the prize; it was getting clinical hours and testing my research hypothesis on how nonprofit agencies operated depending on sizes and duration.

Foster care work is tricky. It was the kind of social work that requires someone with people skills. If one wants to understand the delicate balance of professionalism and work ethics among stakeholders, this is a good starting point. Foster care agencies will challenge one's interpersonal skills in a workplace. It is political at times. It is complicated and complex most of the time. It is emotionally draining all the time. You are pretty much on your own most of the time. Some of these nonprofit agencies tend to have a higher turnover rate than non-foster care, non-mental health-focused ones. I stayed on for almost a year before I felt burnt out and had to move on. I would not exchange this experience for anything else. However, having said this, I don't ever want to do it again.

More Social Work Jobs

My second social work job was with another nonprofit agency. It was somewhat an ideal job. I got to have a caseload and manage staff. I also got to expand the behavioral health program for the agency. I had been on the job for three months and it was at the time of my three-month evaluation when I felt more oppressed and paralyzed. I saw barriers all over and at every angle. Besides enjoying working with kids, I was feeling trapped and discovered again a limited way out in terms of improving my working conditions except to develop another exit strategy. I was planning on how to get away with minimal damage to the relationship. I have tried during my career to leave employers with some professional and cordial impression. I knew I would have to run at some point. The question was how long I was willing to tolerate it before I had to decide if I wanted to be insane or get out in time before that happened. I didn't have an emotional breakdown but came too close a few times in my life and most of these were during the MSW program and working with youth.

While plunging forward with this job, I also developed exit strategies. However, this time these exit strategies involved going back to school. Yes, I have been in college for 27 years, and I was heading back to take two classes, online education this time. I just completed a Child and Adolescent Needs and Strengths (CANS) and California Law and Ethics Exam (one of two required tests to be a licensed clinical social worker). I would have to take another test and that is the California Basic Educational Skills Test (CBEST), a partial fulfillment for pupil

personnel credential (PPSC). The application for the PPSC program involved three letters of recommendation, personal statement, CV, and official transcript. I had asked to waive field hours, so another evaluation form needed to be filled out by a field instructor. Some parts proved difficult for my previous field instructor since I had her several years back. This was extra work for me, but it was worth my time and mental energy. This approach to secure my sanity in terms of seeking options may not be for everyone; I have discovered that by developing exit strategies when things appear to go wrong with work, I tend to become more productive and motivated to fix the problems at hand that have impacted my ability to perform the job.

What is an Ideal job?

My destination is not written in stone, but there was a strong feeling that my place is in academia and research. I have started this process while doing all the things, including publishing my thesis and volunteering as coeditor for a peer-reviewed journal, to secure a competitive slot someday soon in academia. I have a five-year plan to return to academia and that time came up about five years ago or at least my full-time job as a researcher ended five years earlier. I was slightly out of touch with what the latest issues were in academia, including what was happening in professional training in my field as an anthropologist. Having confessed to not working as a researcher, I did not mean that I had stopped conducting research studies or being an anthropologist. I have kept field

More Social Work Jobs

My second social work job was with another nonprofit agency. It was somewhat an ideal job. I got to have a caseload and manage staff. I also got to expand the behavioral health program for the agency. I had been on the job for three months and it was at the time of my three-month evaluation when I felt more oppressed and paralyzed. I saw barriers all over and at every angle. Besides enjoying working with kids, I was feeling trapped and discovered again a limited way out in terms of improving my working conditions except to develop another exit strategy. I was planning on how to get away with minimal damage to the relationship. I have tried during my career to leave employers with some professional and cordial impression. I knew I would have to run at some point. The question was how long I was willing to tolerate it before I had to decide if I wanted to be insane or get out in time before that happened. I didn't have an emotional breakdown but came too close a few times in my life and most of these were during the MSW program and working with youth.

While plunging forward with this job, I also developed exit strategies. However, this time these exit strategies involved going back to school. Yes, I have been in college for 27 years, and I was heading back to take two classes, online education this time. I just completed a Child and Adolescent Needs and Strengths (CANS) and California Law and Ethics Exam (one of two required tests to be a licensed clinical social worker). I would have to take another test and that is the California Basic Educational Skills Test (CBEST), a partial fulfillment for pupil

personnel credential (PPSC). The application for the PPSC program involved three letters of recommendation, personal statement, CV, and official transcript. I had asked to waive field hours, so another evaluation form needed to be filled out by a field instructor. Some parts proved difficult for my previous field instructor since I had her several years back. This was extra work for me, but it was worth my time and mental energy. This approach to secure my sanity in terms of seeking options may not be for everyone; I have discovered that by developing exit strategies when things appear to go wrong with work, I tend to become more productive and motivated to fix the problems at hand that have impacted my ability to perform the job.

What is an Ideal job?

My destination is not written in stone, but there was a strong feeling that my place is in academia and research. I have started this process while doing all the things, including publishing my thesis and volunteering as coeditor for a peer-reviewed journal, to secure a competitive slot someday soon in academia. I have a five-year plan to return to academia and that time came up about five years ago or at least my full-time job as a researcher ended five years earlier. I was slightly out of touch with what the latest issues were in academia, including what was happening in professional training in my field as an anthropologist. Having confessed to not working as a researcher, I did not mean that I had stopped conducting research studies or being an anthropologist. I have kept field

More Social Work Jobs

My second social work job was with another nonprofit agency. It was somewhat an ideal job. I got to have a caseload and manage staff. I also got to expand the behavioral health program for the agency. I had been on the job for three months and it was at the time of my three-month evaluation when I felt more oppressed and paralyzed. I saw barriers all over and at every angle. Besides enjoying working with kids, I was feeling trapped and discovered again a limited way out in terms of improving my working conditions except to develop another exit strategy. I was planning on how to get away with minimal damage to the relationship. I have tried during my career to leave employers with some professional and cordial impression. I knew I would have to run at some point. The question was how long I was willing to tolerate it before I had to decide if I wanted to be insane or get out in time before that happened. I didn't have an emotional breakdown but came too close a few times in my life and most of these were during the MSW program and working with youth.

While plunging forward with this job, I also developed exit strategies. However, this time these exit strategies involved going back to school. Yes, I have been in college for 27 years, and I was heading back to take two classes, online education this time. I just completed a Child and Adolescent Needs and Strengths (CANS) and California Law and Ethics Exam (one of two required tests to be a licensed clinical social worker). I would have to take another test and that is the California Basic Educational Skills Test (CBEST), a partial fulfillment for pupil

personnel credential (PPSC). The application for the PPSC program involved three letters of recommendation, personal statement, CV, and official transcript. I had asked to waive field hours, so another evaluation form needed to be filled out by a field instructor. Some parts proved difficult for my previous field instructor since I had her several years back. This was extra work for me, but it was worth my time and mental energy. This approach to secure my sanity in terms of seeking options may not be for everyone; I have discovered that by developing exit strategies when things appear to go wrong with work, I tend to become more productive and motivated to fix the problems at hand that have impacted my ability to perform the job.

What is an Ideal job?

My destination is not written in stone, but there was a strong feeling that my place is in academia and research. I have started this process while doing all the things, including publishing my thesis and volunteering as coeditor for a peer-reviewed journal, to secure a competitive slot someday soon in academia. I have a five-year plan to return to academia and that time came up about five years ago or at least my full-time job as a researcher ended five years earlier. I was slightly out of touch with what the latest issues were in academia, including what was happening in professional training in my field as an anthropologist. Having confessed to not working as a researcher, I did not mean that I had stopped conducting research studies or being an anthropologist. I have kept field

notes in moleskin notebooks and continued to write papers and review others' manuscripts in related fields (public health, environmental, and refugee health). Now that the plan was in action right after graduation, I was marching toward that finish line by preparing and submitting job applications and related documents to various academic institutions starting fall 2017. However, my exit strategies never precluded another exit strategy whether that was in academia or in the real world. I felt the need to have a foot in each place (one in academia and one out of it). I applied, for example, for primary/secondary school-based jobs to work as a social worker in case I failed to get an offer from an academic institution since I was bound by geographical location at the time.

One thing for sure about having a professional degree is that it is different from a job in academia. One can have an easier time to have that ideal job in a social work field. A degree in anthropology is limited to teaching at a university or working as a contractor for companies that focus on developing a piece of land or government entities trying to understand the impact of development. I must confess that one would learn quickly what one likes or dislikes about a job. Having said this, I feel the need to provide my definition of a professional career versus a job. I am not giving this dichotomy to make a judgment about having a job versus having a career. I am making a distinction to ensure an easier way to communicate my points effectively. My definition of a professional career involves extensive training, such as being a social worker (two or three plus years of training resulting in a degree), a medical doctor (four years of school beyond undergrad degree plus internships/residency), or an attorney (three years of law school plus studying for bar exams). While a job requires some skills and shorter training commitment (which can involve quick training from 6 months to 18 months or on the job learning), a long investment in time and finances is needed for a professional career.

Having an ideal job is difficult to pinpoint since it requires years of trials and errors in working at different positions. I believe in my case that I have come to understand what I generally like to spend time doing. I have always been interested in writing and researching but talking was something else. After spending the last thirty years working at many types of jobs, I realized that what inspires me and drives my motivation is really in writing and reading. A world that I can create and get lost in is what makes me or forces me to feel less guilty to spend time away from my family.

At the time of writing this ethnography, I had started the final job for this research project before I would take the clinical exam. I took the California laws and ethnics exam because it was required to maintain my active status as a clinical social worker and because it was required for accruing the clinical hours. I passed. It was in many ways a relief to have taken part 1 of the exam. Also, I was fortunate to have to do one exam. The clinical exam was going to be a long road. I needed 3000 hours. This rule was changed several years after I completed my MSW degree. The Board of Behavioral Sciences (BBS) used to require 3200 hours. The only barrier now is the clinical exam. I decided to make the third job as a social worker my last and final generalist position because I was working at a school. I wanted to explore psychotherapy work for the remaining time before the hard deadline to return to academia to gain more clinical experience. Beside documentation, I did not see much difficulty in doing the work. Kids do have problems but not in the way of a teenager who would fire me more often than not before they trusted me and I began providing treatment. I also decided that if I could not return to academia, the second best option would be a social work position with a school district because of the summer vacation and winter time off. But most importantly, I had a good clinical supervisor. I liked her personality and her insight into people's experiences. She worked for a school district for over 25 years before retirement. A good clinical supervisor goes a long way. I was still uncertain if school social work was ideal or if returning to academia would be better. I have not had a straight road in terms of a career. My career path seems to go up and down, and most of the time sideways and backwards in many ways, and now perhaps may move forward toward writing, researching, and publishing.

Conclusion

I focused on finding an ideal job. While searching for one, I discussed how all these different experiences help to fine-tune skills and career interests. I concluded by stating that I have yet to get where I need to go. I am still exploring.

The next chapter will focus on specialized areas of social work. I will discuss what each subfield entails and highlight some of the skills needed to ensure success when working in these subfields.

CHAPTER 9

Subfields in Social Work

There are subfields and specializations in the social work discipline, but this part in most training programs appears to be generally abstract to students, at least based on my own experience. Some programs stay with the general training in social work as opposed to identifying one special area except in a hybrid program, which I am now teaching in. Its focus is on behavioral training. However, self-supported programs tend to place more emphasis on specialized training (e.g., a behavioral health focused program), which requires potential students to have some experiences in the field prior to applying. Specialized training in social work seems to be more available through employment or through continuing education than through the varied social work programs. I am more familiar with the four subfields in anthropology since I spent almost fifteen years attending college to obtain a PhD degree in medical anthropology. I only have a master's degree in social work and limited research experience of what constitutes social work research. I noticed one striking difference in the social work field, and that is the distinction between mental health and non-mental health areas. These were the two routes offered as areas of specialization in the social work program that I was in.

Because the emphasis is on concentration, I have listed below some areas that I have had some exposure to and can have a conversation about:

- Mental health
- Forensic social work
- School social work
- Medical social work
- Foster care (families, children, and youth)

Each of these areas of work required different types of mental capacity and levels of tolerance and maturity. I also wanted to emphasize that one's own personality and personal beliefs can contribute to whether there is a fit in the job and the clients one serves. I know that certain areas of social work require a lot of engaging with stakeholders. Child welfare is an example. It requires one's careful interactions with people, which determines one's success. While in this case, success means lasting more than eighteen months before feeling burnt out on the job. I had some jobs that I felt burnt out after three months; generally those that involved child protective services (CPS) or related positions.

CPS work is tricky in a sense that it goes beyond a typical social worker's work. It is not about one's own effective treatment plans and/or therapeutic relationship with clients. Knowing the clients is not adequate in addressing their needs if one cannot get all the other service providers in line to have a unified response. Foster care is one of those areas that involves many individuals, including attorneys, court assigned mentors, county case social workers, nonprofit agency case managers, families, foster parents, case coordinators, etc. Almost all key players have distinct personalities, and some are not easy to deal with. Sometimes, but not always, they can be the barriers, not the solutions.

According to the Bureau of Labor Statistics, the estimate for employment in children, family, and school social work was 298,840 in May 2016 with a mean annual wage of $47,510.[xxv] The industries with the highest employment are individual and family services, state government, local government, elementary and secondary schools, and outpatient care centers, according to the 2016 Bureau of Labor Statistics. The top paying industries are elementary and secondary schools, other schools, and instruction, business/professional, labor, political, and similar organizations, management/scientific and technical consulting services, and local government agencies.

The average wage for a state government position was $46,970 compared to local government at $54,210. The highest average wage was with elementary and secondary schools with average wage of $62,170 compared to community food and housing, emergency, and other relief services at $37,840.

Generally, the average wage is a lot lower in a nonprofit agency that is relatively small (less than 150 staff) compared to a big system like Kaiser or Sutter Health or similar nonprofit medical facilities. The bigger nonprofit agencies are more established, and their pay is comparable to that of the federal, state, and local government. Then there is pay differential due to whether one is living in urban or rural areas or in states that have a lower cost of living and less demands for social work services. Also, one's previous professional experience can have an impact on one's salary. Once a social worker is licensed, though, this changes one's salary levels greatly. One can negotiate for a better rate and to a certain extent tell potential employers. So, citing statistics alone does not give us much information about financial compensation.

Mental Health

A social worker can work in many settings. If one is interested in mental health social work, one is more likely to end up in hospitals, nursing homes, assisted living facilities, substance abuse treatment centers, or home health agencies. Mental health social work is psychology-centric; to borrow a phrase used by a VA field instructor, meaning the focus is on psychotherapy as opposed to general social services. Mental health social workers' focus is to empower individuals with mental illness—and their families, careers, and communities—to lead fulfilling, independent lives. One of the best ways to gauge salaries is through looking at job announcements on Indeed. It gives one a better idea of what one probably will make with a master's degree in social work. The Alameda Alliance for Health listed a range between $58,760 and $88,150 per year. This is a medical setting. Job duties are like any medical setting including the government agencies. The question becomes personal interests, with work. I discovered that a combination of case management, counseling and therapy works best. It reduces monotony and allows for a more comprehensive approach to intervention and treatment.

Forensic Social Work

Forensic social work seems to be on the forefront of interesting social work, at least at the time in which I was still in training. I had a classmate whose case presentations focused on the safety of professionals and service providers. The prison systems hire forensic social workers. It is one of the industries where funding is not of a major concern (I will discuss further in the next chapter). Forensic social workers can find jobs in juvenile detention centers, prisons, or jails. These places offer great benefits and decent financial compensations. When I was a lot younger, benefits were not as important as the salary. More vacation time, for example, becomes more important as I am now aging and want to spend more time with my family. Prison work is difficult and dangerous at times.

At the time of writing this ethnography, my immediate supervisor used to work for a prison. She lasted eight months. She said it was generally scary being small and a female. One unintentional look at someone might cause danger to one's life. The job duties were limited to liability, for example, conducting a quick assessment to determine if an inmate is suicidal or homicidal. She said it was not about treatment or rehabilitation at all. She spent five minutes per inmate. The burnout rate can be high with the notion of feeling under constant threat. No need to ask about vicarious trauma in this case. It is clear and present.

The California Department of Corrections and Rehabilitation, for example, recruits social workers and places them at their health and correctional facilities. Since social workers are not psychologists whose primary job is to conduct assessments, a social worker's role in prison is to conduct various forms of group and individual therapy, make recommendations on admission, transfer, parole, discharge, and therapeutic activities, and to select, administer, and interpret personality intelligence. They are also hired to conduct psychological tests and consult with medical personnel regarding findings of medical examinations. A recent job posting listed an annual salary of $68,628 for a non-licensed social worker and $73,824 for licensed.[xxvi] A big system like the prison comes with established, non-negotiable salary cap or salary ranges. However, if one were to be hired as supervisor, the annual salary range is between $91,392 and $107,112. In this case, one would have a wiggle room to negotiate. Of course, if an institution wants you, then things do change. I suppose one would have leverage.

School Social Work

From my own experience, school social work is the best to work if one has children in primary schools and prefers a calmer working environment. This does not mean that one does not run into difficult situations. If one were to work at an elementary school setting, lots of interventions require either play therapy or art therapy. Children will talk when children want to talk, so playing along with them helps ease into conversations about their own challenges. It takes a different skill set. It takes patience, again, in a different way than with teenagers. I had the opportunity to work at various levels from elementary to middle to high school. Working with teenagers can be extremely tough, especially in an urban setting. In addition to poverty and family dysfunctions, there are other external factors that are generally summed up as the impact of trauma (urban community and family violence) on families and substance abuse. Drugs are a big problem in both rural and urban poor communities.

There is one barrier or challenge if one wants to work for a school. One will need to get a credential called Pupil Personnel Service Credential (PPSC) to be employed by a school district or otherwise one would need to work for a school but be employed through a nonprofit agency. There are disadvantages working for a nonprofit agency. Not all of them follow the school calendar, meaning that one cannot take time off when schools are out. One will need to follow the agency's policies and benefit package. In my case, for example, I had two weeks off per year. That was after I worked for one year (one can accrue hours as one works). But the advantage is that one can start immediately and gain school social work experience. Nonprofit agencies can hire someone to fill a position immediately or as short term as two or three weeks. As a beginner in the social work field, one can get to be in the field and start a career as a school social worker immediately. One can take this time while working at a school setting to get your PPSC. PPSC requires two courses (school social work and school laws/ethics) generally but some schools have different requirements.

I enjoy working for a school because children have a blank slate in which to instill positive change. Providing interventions this early on in life can have profound effects when they grow up. They are young and they can still learn. The annual salary ranges from about $43,000 to $75,000 as a school social worker. The upper end is usually for those who already have licenses (MFT/LCSW). If you are hired directly by the school district, though, in addition to time off during the school calendar, your salary ranges between $50,000 and $87,000. The Sacramento City School District pays social workers an annual salary of $54,400, for example. This comes with ten months of work, not twelve months. The San Francisco School District has a range of $58,000 to $85,000 per annum. It is a ten-month work period. Of course, there are more desirable places to work beside the Oakland Bay such as Hawaii or Florida if one likes warmer climates. Hawaii pays school social workers a lot less. One job announcement with the Department of Education listed at an annum of $60,000 maximum for a 12-month period, not for ten months like some of the schools in the San Francisco Bay Area. Other islands such as Maui or Hawaii pay about the same if not a little less. One gets the benefit of living on an island and may feel like one is on a vacation all the time. This may be worth it since one's mental health is also important.

Medical Social Work

Medical social work seems interesting overall. I had limited experience. I spent one academic year at a VA medical facility inside a methadone clinic. I cannot tell if I like the work or hate it. This is where the experience with a field instructor plays a critical role in the way one gains the experience (I discussed this in detail in Chapter 7). If a hospital causes anxiety, medical social work may not be a good fit; however, there is an incentive to work as a medical social worker at a hospital. In places such as Kaiser, VA medical facilities, and children's hospitals, the financial compensations and benefits cannot be beaten by other industries. In the Oakland Bay Area, children's hospitals provide health benefits for the entire family at no cost to the employee. This is unbeatable if one has children and if one is a single parent. Health benefits are expensive, ranging about $1,000/month to $2,000 depending on what type of industry one is working for. In a foster care nonprofit agency, for example, my medical subsidies for a family can be as high as $2,000 a month and my salary per annum is about $48,000. Now, you do the math. But with medical settings such as big nonprofit hospitals, the salary ranges between $60,000 and $90,000. If one is looking for supervisory positions and one is licensed, one can negotiate for a lot more.

There is something to be said about a medical facility. It is stressful and can be intimidating to work in. People go to a hospital because they are not feeling well and that is why they seek medical help. So, having said this, working in such an environment requires a different personality. If one is not into dealing with people with illness and trauma (new wounds), medical social work might be tough. I like to say that we have a PhD degree in our own bodies. In other words, no one knows you better than you. You know the kind of work you feel most fit or comfortable with. It just takes time to explore what works best.

Foster Care and Case Management

Foster care was a big business when I was in the MSW program from 2014 to 2016. There were funding sources to pay for graduate students, for example, Title IVE, which are federal financial aid funds. Of course, there is no such thing as a free ride. There is a commitment after the degree of two years in a government child welfare position. This is not a bad trade if one prefers this commitment over taking out loans. Foster care is hard work, which I discussed elsewhere in this ethnography. Complexity is the only characterization in this type of work. The pay is not there either. A recent graduate with a master's degree in social work can expect to earn between $43,000 and $54,000 per annum. The work schedule is flexible. One works generally off site or at home and in the field to meet clients. The good part about this type of work is that it is flexible. The only disadvantage is the low pay, but again, the flexibility in schedule is desirable for some people with children and other obligations. I worked in this position for about 10 months but intermittently. There are plenty of foster care and child welfare positions. If one wants something fast, this is one area of social work that one can get employment quickly. The burnout rates are high in this line of work. Foster care issues are serious and complex, as children are taken away from their families because of abuse, neglect, or something more gruesome. For example, I came across a case with a six-month-old girl who was raped by an immediate family member. I did not think this was possible. One can get sick by what one learns about the depth of despair from learning the evil of certain human beings in our society. I used to think that people are capable of being bad but are not generally evil. The foster care experience informed me otherwise. I am convinced that some people are naturally evil. This perspective changes the way I see social work and my practice. There is the professional side that craves for deeper and more profound work, but there is the vulnerable me that prefers a safer route.

Conclusion

In this chapter, I discussed the different areas of concentration or subfields to shed light on the kind of social work that is available out there. Although my experience in social work is limited to certain areas of social work, I do believe that exposure to any of these areas can offer insight into future work. One cannot know for sure unless one tries different areas of social work to get a sense of what fits one best. I also discussed salaries in different industries and who is hiring is more in the field. I also offered pros and cons in the varied areas.

The next chapter focuses on bigger systems. I will compare a government entity and a nonprofit system by highlighting some issues relating to big systems, such as bureaucracies and office politics. Finally, I will touch on what works for someone who prefers to be practical like me or who likes engaging in office politics and having power.

CHAPTER 10

Big Systems

The big systems tend to have a lot of bureaucracies and power-competing structures/leadership. The consequence is often on the receiving end. Staff gets lost in it. Patients and clients tend to get overwhelmed due to its mere size. The big systems take a long time to get someone hired and there isn't much flexibility in the hiring practices, benefits, or salary negotiations. Everything tends to be standardized and follows a hierarchical system that has been put in place and at times unchangeable unless something terrible happens (e.g., patient waiting time at the VA). The VA has serious problems with backlog where patients waited in some cases over a year for service. The VA is a complex system, which I will discuss in detail next.

The VA/Federal Government

The Veterans Affairs is a big system. In fact, it is the second largest government agency. According to its website, the VA health administration provides care at 1,243 health care facilities, including 170 medical centers, and 1,063 outpatient sites.[xxvii] They serve about 9 million people per year. Its budget is huge. I have seen numbers ($180 billion), and it employs over 340,000 people. In addition to its size, the VA must address its diverse needs of its 6 million patients.[xxviii] The last twenty years of wars (namely in Iraq and Afghanistan) have taken a toll on the system despite its huge budget and resources. They are facing an aging population of patients, post-war consequences of having veterans with battle-broken bodies and emotional wounds.

At the time I wrote this ethnography, we faced an extraordinary time with the White House under the leadership of Donald Trump. He signed the Veteran Appeals Improvement and Modernization Act of 2017 to fix some of the problems. Another solution was to upgrade their IT system. None of these changes would do much to change a big system such as this. It takes time and money. Their hiring process remains unchanged. If one wants to work for the VA, one will have to carefully fix their resume and precisely follow the instructions on the website. Once somebody or something determines that one meets all requirements, one will receive an email stating a time for an interview. Like the county and state, appointments for interviews are unchangeable. One will have to take time or cancel other obligations to make room for the interview. I did not have the patience to wait to accommodate this type of system. I tried several times and failed to follow through because of other obligations.

Another way of looking at this is that there are many benefits in working for a big system. One benefit is the financial compensation. One can make enough to live somewhat comfortably compared to other social work positions (nonprofit agencies are notorious for not paying well). So, one just needs to focus on their position instead of having to work elsewhere to supplement their income to live or pay bills. The second benefit is that one does not have to worry about looking for another job or a time-limited contract. Nonprofits get time-limited contracts and are subject to annual renewals that are contingent on performance. In addition, benefits in places like the VA are generous.

The County

I have limited experience with the county system but know enough to say that the county functions like the VA. The difference is that some practices are outdated, especially with units that have a low turnover rate of employment. But one usually finds an older or aging workforce. People stay for thirty or forty years. So, their degrees and professional practices are from decades prior. One will have issues with coworkers and other professionals if one is a recent graduate with more up-to-date education. One county unit that I have become familiar with did not care about staff productivity. The leadership cared more about how well one got along with coworkers instead of how hard they tried to help clients. That was one of the negative comments that I received while working in one unit in a local county agency. The supervisor's critique was that I chose to spend time taking care of clients instead of socializing with my coworkers. Five years later, I encountered two ex-clients at a grocery store who thanked me for finding them an apartment. They told me that they did not want to die at a hostel or shelter, and they had been going to the county unit for over two years and no one helped them the way I did. Because they did not want to lose their apartment, they got themselves a job and got out of general assistance.

I do not have much to say about the county. I am sure some people find it rewarding. I have relatives who worked for a county for twenty or thirty years. They had no problem. But they told me that they feared doing something that would cause their jobs such as speaking out about something that needs changing or improvement. They agreed to everything that their supervisors said or told them. Conformity appeared to be more important to the local government agencies than staff performance. A county job tends to pay well and comes with good benefits. This is the upside. Plus, one does not have to worry about losing one's job because of funding cuts or grants not being renewed.

Funding Concerns

After I graduated with my BA degree from UC Berkeley, I was employed as a community youth counselor. The federal grant was for three years. I remembered at the beginning of the final year I was nervous over the prospect that I might have to seek unemployment. At the time, I was more interested in pursuing graduate school than looking for another job. The prospect of both scared me at the time. I was in my early twenties. Uncertainties seemed so daunting. I was young and having a secure job was a priority. But I did not have that option then. Because both options required taking actions. I chose the latter. I took the opportunity to apply to graduate schools instead of looking for another job. But the feeling of losing a job was not great. I did not know how many nights I lost sleep from that first job after college. So, working for the government will help with financial securities, but such a job will take time since bureaucracies tend to dictate the hiring process. The shortest time that I've heard, including based on my own experience, was three months from submitting application to hiring. One colleague told me it took him three years to get hired by a local government agency. I believe it was a city, not county job. He was happy to have the job in the end.

If one is doing direct services, sometimes one gets away from having to worry about funding. However, an honest nonprofit agency would try to let the candidate know in advance if the contract is coming to an end or if the contract is about to be renewed. This is not always the case. One never knows for sure until one is hired. This was the case with me. I was told after I was hired with one job that I had three months and that I should help the agency with the grant proposals and to look for other funding sources.

Gaining Professional Experience: A Steppingstone

What is good about working for a nonprofit agency? It is a good steppingstone toward one's career. While one fishes for a bigger fish (a more secure position), one can try to gain professional experience at the same time through learning everything about the position. As I indicated in this ethnography in various chapters, I worked for several nonprofit agencies before I felt settled in one. I lasted only a few months for couple of them even though it was not intentional. I would stay if I felt that it was a good fit. However, most were not a good fit. I did not like the culture, practices, or the people in them. But each experience in these nonprofit agencies shed light onto the kinds of experience that I needed and the skills I should have to make me competitive with future opportunities.

If one thinks that the glass is half full, one is less likely to be disappointed. It took me a long time to realize that I was not wasting my time and that I was gaining something valuable even though I did not always see it at the time. I later learned that the best way to assess what I learned was to contemplate and put on my 20/20 vision to see the goodness in the experience instead of dwelling on negative past experiences. This helps me to better understand my needs and follow that ideal dream job. So, the moral part of the story is that one can take any small experience and learn to see the value in it.

Conclusion

This chapter focused on personal and professional experiences of working for a big system. I discussed advantages and disadvantages of working for a big system. I also compared the differences between two big systems and to those of a small nonprofit agency. I also discussed benefits and job securities in these systems.

Epilogue

By the time this ethnography was complete, I was already back in academia and fully immersed in clinical exam prep. Fires were the worst in California in 2020. We experienced darkness for an entire fall day as a result and we were told to stay in door for weeks due to a dangerous level of air quality. Donald Trump lost the election. Joe Biden was elected as the next president. COVID-19 killed over 500,000 Americans. I remembered watching the number of new cases daily. It felt unreal at the time. I was fully vaccinated, and my university was in a planning mode for a 51% repopulation of the campus.

By the time this ethnography went to my editor, it was one year from Governor Gavin Newsom ordering shelter in place and some signs of normalcy have returned as the summer approaches. The number of new cases dropped to 389 in California with 2 deaths (June 1, 2021), compared to the peak of at least 40,000 cases daily in early December 2020. The United States is looking hopeful. China saw an uptick of new cases. The worry now is with those who refused to be vaccinated. Vaccination rates varied with CA, reaching 70% while others are still struggling at 30%. Ohio is using a lottery of $1 million to encourage people to vaccinate. Some offer tickets to sports events, beers, or wines.

I am prepping for a tenure and promotion application this summer. I am due to submit my materials by Sept. 3, 2021. I am also studying for the license exam in social work. I never let go of one thing that defined me. I still go for job interviews, mostly academic positions. I even had interviews for two straight years for the same job and made it all the way for the final phase, but the university retracted its position both times. The first was due to the COVID-19 shutdown, but the second time was due to the lack of candidates. I also turned down an academic job. I still have interviews to go to as I am done writing this ethnography. Exit strategies seem to be a coping strategy for me. I am not looking to move or change jobs.

Resources
Clinical Hours
3000 hours
Associate Clinical Social Worker or Associate Social Worker (ACSW/ASW)

As soon as you received your degree, you can register with the Board of Behavioral Science if you live in California.

PPSC

How it worked for me was the PPSC Program at the university offered the pupil personnel service credential. Credential analysts at the SJSU look over the application and will submit to the appropriate entity. The California Commission on Teacher Credentialing online account starts with:

1) Go to www.ctc.ca.gov if you live in California. Click on the Educator Login

2) Create/log in to your personal profile on the secure Educator page

3) Enter your SSN and Date of Birth to begin creating your User ID and password

4) Enter your personal information including your selection of a User ID and Password

5) After creating your User ID and Password, you will be directed back to the login screen to use your User ID and

Password. Continue to follow the prompt after you press continue.

450 hours (250 elementary schools and 200 hours high school)

2 classes (Law and Ethics in Social Work/Social Work in School Setting)

Submitting

Law & Ethics Exam

One needs to pass the Law & Ethics Exam before one can sign up for the clinical exam. This is a two-process approach. The approval of 3000 clinical hours is through Board of Behavioral Sciences (BBS). The second part of the exam is through the National Association of Social Workers (NASW). Once BBS approved the hours, one will receive a letter from ASW.

Clinical Social Work Exam

I am prepping for the exam now. I started two years ago, but I had to abandon the prep time for other obligations. Most recently, COVID-19 put a stop to this process. I took quizzes to prep for the actual exam. These quizzes are organized into two major areas: 1) Ethics & Law; and 2) Clinical Knowledge.

References

About Recreational Therapy. NCTRC. (n.d.). https://nctrc.org/about-ncrtc/about-recreational-therapy/.

Administration, V. H. (2008, April 29). *Veterans Affairs*. VA.gov Home. https://va.gov/health/.

American Psychological Association. (2017, July). *What Is Exposure Therapy?* American Psychological Association. http://www.apa.org/ptsd-guideline/patients-and-families/exposure-therapy.aspx.

Bremner, J. D. (2006). Traumatic stress: effects on the brain. *Dialogues in Clinical Neuroscience, 8*(4), 445–461. https://doi.org/10.31887/dcns.2006.8.4/jbremner

Chapman, A. L. (2006). Dialectical Behavior Therapy: Current Indications and Unique Elements. *Psychiatry (Edgmont), 3*(9), 62–68.

Chaves County CASA. (2020, September 19). https://casakids.org/.

D'Cruz, H., Gillingham, P., & Melendez, S. (2006). Reflexivity, its Meanings and Relevance for Social Work: A Critical Review of the Literature. *British Journal of Social Work, 37*(1), 73–90. https://doi.org/10.1093/bjsw/bcl001

Dhikav, V., & Anand, K. S. (2012). Hippocampus in health and disease: An overview. *Annals of Indian Academy of Neurology, 15*(4), 239–246. https://doi.org/10.4103/0972-2327.104323

Gallagher, M., & Chiba, A. A. (1996). The amygdala and emotion. *Current Opinion in Neurobiology, 6*(2), 221–227. https://doi.org/10.1016/s0959-4388(96)80076-6

Introduction to Self-Care. University at Buffalo School of Social Work - University at Buffalo. (2018, September 13). https://socialwork.buffalo.edu/resources/self-care-starter-kit/introduction-to-self-care.html.

Job Posting: Clinical Social Worker. Job Posting. (n.d.). https://jobs.ca.gov/CalHrPublic/Jobs/JobPostingPrint.aspx?jcid=80511.

King, R., & O'Brien, T. (2011). Transference and countertransference: Opportunities and risks as two technical constructs migrate beyond their psychoanalytic homeland. *Psychotherapy in Australia*, *17*(4), 12–17.

Landreth, G. L. (2012). *Play therapy: the art of the relationship*. Routledge.

Mayo Foundation for Medical Education and Research. (2019, March 19). *Chronic stress puts your health at risk*. Mayo Clinic. https://www.mayoclinic.org/healthy-lifestyle/stress-management/in-depth/stress/art-20046037.

Perishable. (n.d.). *YAbout IPT*. IPT Institute. https://iptinstitute.com/about-ipt/.

Pleger, B., Ruff, C. C., Blankenburg, F., Klöppel, S., Driver, J., & Dolan, R. J. (2009). Influence of Dopaminergically Mediated Reward on Somatosensory Decision-Making. *PLoS Biology*, *7*(7). https://doi.org/10.1371/journal.pbio.1000164

Rowland-Klein, D., & Dunlop, R. (1998). The Transmission of Trauma across Generations: Identification with Parental Trauma in Children of Holocaust Survivors. *Australian & New Zealand Journal of Psychiatry*, *32*(3), 358–369. https://doi.org/10.3109/00048679809065528

Sapolsky, R. M. (2001). Depression, antidepressants, and the shrinking hippocampus. *Proceedings of the National Academy of Sciences*, *98*(22), 12320–12322. https://doi.org/10.1073/pnas.231475998

Seeking Safety. Treatment Innovations. (n.d.). http://www.treatment-innovations.org/seeking-safety.html.

Steele, J. (2017, January 2). *4 biggest issues facing next Veterans Affairs secretary*. Tribune. http://www.sandiegouniontribune.com/military/the-intel/sd-me-va-priorities-20161230-story.html.

Teffer, K., & Semendeferi, K. (2012). Human prefrontal cortex. *Evolution of the Primate Brain*, 191–218. https://doi.org/10.1016/b978-0-444-53860-4.00009-x

U.S. Bureau of Labor Statistics. (2017, March 31). *21-1021 Child, Family, and School Social Workers*. U.S. Bureau of Labor Statistics. https://www.bls.gov/oes/2016/may/oes211021.htm.

U.S. Department of Health and Human Services. (n.d.). *Borderline Personality Disorder*. National Institute of Mental Health. https://www.nimh.nih.gov/health/topics/borderline-personality-disorder/index.shtml.

What is Cognitive Behavior Therapy: Beck Institute. Beck Institute for Cognitive Behavior Therapy. (n.d.). https://beckinstitute.org/get-informed/what-is-cognitive-therapy/.

White, J. B., Langer, E. J., Yariv, L., & Welch, J. C. (2006). Frequent Social Comparisons and Destructive Emotions and Behaviors: The Dark Side of Social Comparisons. *Journal of Adult Development*, 13(1), 36–44. https://doi.org/10.1007/s10804-006-9005-0

Yong, E. (2021, May 3). The world's smallest fly probably decapitates really tiny ants. Science. https://www.nationalgeographic.com/science/article/the-worlds-smallest-fly-probably-decapitates-really-tiny-ants.

Young, I. (2004). Five Faces of Oppression. In P. O'Connor & L. Heldke (Eds.), Oppression, privilege, and resistance: theoretical perspectives on racism, sexism, and heterosexism. essay, McGraw-Hill.

FOOTNOTES

---

[i] American Psychological Association. (2017, July). *What Is Exposure Therapy?* American Psychological Association. http://www.apa.org/ptsd-guideline/patients-and-families/exposure-therapy.aspx.

[ii] *Seeking Safety. Treatment Innovations.* (n.d.). http://www.treatment-innovations.org/seeking-safety.html.

[iii] Landreth, G. L. (2012). Play therapy: the art of the relationship. Routledge.

[iv] Chaves County CASA. (2020, September 19). https://casakids.org/.

[v] D'Cruz, H., Gillingham, P., & Melendez, S. (2006). Reflexivity, its Meanings and Relevance for Social Work: A Critical Review of the Literature. *British Journal of Social Work*, *37*(1), 73–90. https://doi.org/10.1093/bjsw/bcl001

[vi] Bremner, J. D. (2006). Traumatic stress: effects on the brain. *Dialogues in Clinical Neuroscience*, *8*(4), 445–461. https://doi.org/10.31887/dcns.2006.8.4/jbremner

[vii] Gallagher, M., & Chiba, A. A. (1996). The amygdala and emotion. *Current Opinion in Neurobiology*, *6*(2), 221–227. https://doi.org/10.1016/s0959-4388(96)80076-6

[viii] Dhikav, V., & Anand, K. S. (2012). Hippocampus in health and disease: An overview. *Annals of Indian Academy of Neurology*, *15*(4), 239–246. https://doi.org/10.4103/0972-2327.104323

[ix] Sapolsky, R. M. (2001). Depression, antidepressants, and the shrinking hippocampus. *Proceedings of the National Academy of Sciences, 98*(22), 12320–12322. https://doi.org/10.1073/pnas.231475998

[x] Teffer, K., & Semendeferi, K. (2012). Human prefrontal cortex. *Evolution of the Primate Brain*, 191–218. https://doi.org/10.1016/b978-0-444-53860-4.00009-x

[xi] Rowland-Klein, D., & Dunlop, R. (1998). The Transmission of Trauma across Generations: Identification with Parental Trauma in Children of Holocaust Survivors. Australian & *New Zealand Journal of Psychiatry, 32*(3), 358–369. https://doi.org/10.3109/00048679809065528

[xii] King, R., & O'Brien, T. (2011). Transference and countertransference: Opportunities and risks as two technical constructs migrate beyond their psychoanalytic homeland. *Psychotherapy in Australia, 17*(4), 12–17.

[xiii] *Introduction to Self-Care*. University at Buffalo School of Social Work - University at Buffalo. (2018, September 13). https://socialwork.buffalo.edu/resources/self-care-starter-kit/introduction-to-self-care.html.

[xiv] About Recreational Therapy. NCTRC. (n.d.). https://nctrc.org/about-ncrtc/about-recreational-therapy/.

[xv] Bremner, J. D. (2006). Traumatic stress: effects on the brain. *Dialogues in Clinical Neuroscience, 8*(4), 445–461. https://doi.org/10.31887/dcns.2006.8.4/jbremner

[xvi] Mayo Foundation for Medical Education and Research. (2019, March 19*). Chronic stress puts your health at risk*. Mayo Clinic. https://www.mayoclinic.org/healthy-lifestyle/stress-management/in-depth/stress/art-20046037.

[xvii] Pleger, B., Ruff, C. C., Blankenburg, F., Klöppel, S., Driver, J., & Dolan, R. J. (2009). Influence of Dopaminergically Mediated Reward on Somatosensory Decision-Making. *PLoS Biology*, *7*(7). https://doi.org/10.1371/journal.pbio.1000164

[xviii] White, J. B., Langer, E. J., Yariv, L., & Welch, J. C. (2006). Frequent Social Comparisons and Destructive Emotions and Behaviors: The Dark Side of Social Comparisons. *Journal of Adult Development*, *13*(1), 36–44. https://doi.org/10.1007/s10804-006-9005-0

[xix] Yong, E. (2021, May 3). *The world's smallest fly probably decapitates really tiny ants*. Science. https://www.nationalgeographic.com/science/article/the-worlds-smallest-fly-probably-decapitates-really-tiny-ants.

[xx] Young, I. (2004). Five Faces of Oppression. In P. O'Connor & L. Heldke (Eds.), *Oppression, privilege, and resistance: theoretical perspectives on racism, sexism, and heterosexism.* essay, McGraw-Hill.

[xxi] *What is Cognitive Behavior Therapy: Beck Institute*. Beck Institute for Cognitive Behavior Therapy. (n.d.). https://beckinstitute.org/get-informed/what-is-cognitive-therapy/.

[xxii] Perishable. (n.d.). *YAbout IPT*. IPT Institute. https://iptinstitute.com/about-ipt/.

[xxiii] Chapman, A. L. (2006). Dialectical Behavior Therapy: Current Indications and Unique Elements. *Psychiatry (Edgmont), 3*(9), 62–68.

[xxiv] U.S. Department of Health and Human Services. (n.d.). *Borderline Personality Disorder*. National Institute of Mental Health. https://www.nimh.nih.gov/health/topics/borderline-personality-disorder/index.shtml.

[xxv] U.S. Bureau of Labor Statistics. (2017, March 31). *21-1021 Child, Family, and School Social Workers*. U.S. Bureau of Labor Statistics. https://www.bls.gov/oes/2016/may/oes211021.htm.

[xxvi] *Job Posting: Clinical Social Worker*. Job Posting. (n.d.). https://jobs.ca.gov/CalHrPublic/Jobs/JobPostingPrint.aspx?jcid=80511.

[xxvii] Administration, V. H. (2008, April 29). *Veterans Affairs*. VA.gov Home. https://va.gov/health/.

[xxviii] Steele, J. (2017, January 2). *4 biggest issues facing next Veterans Affairs secretary*. Tribune. http://www.sandiegouniontribune.com/military/the-intel/sd-me-va-priorities-20161230-story.html.

www.ingramcontent.com/pod-product-compliance
Lightning Source LLC
LaVergne TN
LVHW091047100526
838202LV00077B/3071